Otis Lee Crenshaw is a country and western musician whose short career ended abruptly when he disappeared near Lake Mead, Arizona, under mysterious circumstances.

His only recorded album, *My Donuts, Goddamn*, sold upwards of a dozen copies and was described in the *Country Music Journal* as an album that 'clearly smacks of someone owing someone else a favour'. He is also the author of Narvel Crump's multi-million-selling hit, 'The Scrabble Song'.

A second album of Otis Lee Crenshaw's songs is due to be released just as soon as he's finished writing them.

Also by Rich Hall

Things Snowball

OTIS LEE CRENSHAW:
I BLAME SOCIETY

RICH HALL

ABACUS

An *Abacus* Original

First published in Great Britain in 2004 by Abacus

A CIP catalogue record for this book
is available from the British Library.

ISBN 0 349 11818 3

Typeset in Palatino by
Palimpsest Book Production Limited,
Polmont, Stirlingshire

Printed and bound in Great Britain by
Clays Ltd, St Ives plc

Abacus
An imprint of
Time Warner Book Group UK
Brettenham House
Lancaster Place
London WC2E 7EN

www.twbg.co.uk

For Karen Eva

Acknowledgements:
Thanks, especially, to Mike Wilmot.
Also, Sean Meo, Andrew Beint, Antonia Hodgson
and, of course, Addison Cresswell.

Foreword

This ain't no autobiography. I don't merit one 'cause I've never done a single goddamn thing to advance civility. But I've got a story or two to tell, and you'll hear about it.

My wives, Brendas every one of 'em, have drifted by me in a fog of bourbonitis. Now and then, there's been moments of clarity and this is what I remember. This is my day in court.

IN THE UNITED STATES COURT OF APPEALS FOR THE SEVENTH CIRCUIT AT KNOXVILLE, TENNESSEE

The United States vs. Otis Lee Crenshaw:
Defendant-Appellant

Appeal from the US District Court for the Seventh
District Court at Knoxville

Judge: Hon. Milton Easterbrook
Representing the Appellant: Mr Crenshaw
chooses to represent himself
Before the Prosecution: David Wendale, US
Attorney

OFFICIAL COURTROOM TRANSCRIPT

JUDGE EASTERBROOK: Mr Crenshaw, you have been convicted in the US District Court for Eastern Tennessee on one count of conspiracy to kidnap the employees of the Bank of Knoxville in violation of 18 USC 612. Is that correct?

OTIS LEE CRENSHAW: Can I make a motion for a mistrial?

JUDGE EASTERBROOK: This isn't a trial. This is a sentencing. Where is your counsel?

OTIS LEE CRENSHAW: I'm representing myself.

JUDGE EASTERBROOK: That's a really bad idea.

OTIS LEE CRENSHAW: So was finding me guilty. This court is full of bad ideas.

JUDGE EASTERBROOK: Very well. You have the right to waive counsel. But I'm warning you now, I will not appoint another attorney if you choose to appeal this sentence at a later date. You have abandoned your discretion in this choice.

OTIS LEE CRENSHAW: I know more about what I did than any lawyer. I was there.

JUDGE EASTERBROOK: On the afternoon in question, you entered the Bank of Knoxville and took several employees hostage.

OTIS LEE CRENSHAW: I didn't take any hostages! I took my shirt off. I yelled a few things. That's it.

JUDGE EASTERBROOK: There are several witnesses to an incriminating utterance about the employees being 'prisoners'. That was the crux of the prosecutor's case.

OTIS LEE CRENSHAW: I did say we were prisoners. But I meant prisoners of debt. Prisoners of the systematic indenture of World Banking practices. Which keeps ordinary people's heads under the water while the tide of advancing interest rates . . .

JUDGE EASTERBROOK: Mr Crenshaw, this isn't the place for your polemics about World Banking. Do you have anything to say before sentencing?

OTIS LEE CRENSHAW: Yes, Your Honor, indeed I do. Ladies and gentlemen of the court . . . 'a man isn't on trial here today. Civilization is on trial!'

JUDGE EASTERBROOK: Mr Crenshaw, what are you doing?

OTIS LEE CRENSHAW: You don't recognize that quote?

JUDGE EASTERBROOK: No.

OTIS LEE CRENSHAW: Well, you should. And you claim to be a learned man of the law.

JUDGE EASTERBROOK: Mr Crenshaw, I'm warning you . . .

OTIS LEE CRENSHAW: Judge Easterbrook, surely you are familiar with the most famous case to ever be tried in this state. I refer, of course, to the Scopes Monkey Trial, which was conducted in 1925 in a courtroom not fifty miles from where we are standing now.

JUDGE EASTERBROOK: I'm not standing. You are.

OTIS LEE CRENSHAW: Be that what it may, Judge Easterbrook, would you remind the court the outcome of that landmark case?

JUDGE EASTERBROOK: Mr Crenshaw, I don't have time for this . . .

OTIS LEE CRENSHAW: Very well, I will do it for you. It was the consensus of the jury that the teaching of evolution in the schools of Tennessee was illegal. The People of Tennessee upheld the argument of the prosecutor, William Jennings Bryant, that man was created in the image of God and did not ascend from monkeys. And in doing so, ruled against Clarence Darrow and his argument for evolution. Wasn't that the outcome, Your Honor?

JUDGE EASTERBROOK: What has that got to do with kidnapping?

OTIS LEE CRENSHAW: Everything! Everything! In the

titanic struggle between good and evil, between truth and ignorance, good and truth won out.

JUDGE EASTERBROOK: Can the histrionics. This is a courtroom, not a stage.

OTIS LEE CRENSHAW: The verdict in that trial stands today. To wit, you and me don't come from no monkeys.

JUDGE EASTERBROOK: Are you done?

OTIS LEE CRENSHAW: Now, Judge, who are you and I to question the veracity of that decision? A decision made by the good, honest, God-fearing people of this Great State of Tennessee. Do you want to be the one who violates that ruling?

JUDGE EASTERBROOK: What do you mean?

OTIS LEE CRENSHAW: I mean, it is against the law in the State of Tennessee to ascend from animals. But if you send me to prison, you will make a mockery of that law.

JUDGE EASTERBROOK: How so?

OTIS LEE CRENSHAW: Because prison will turn me into an animal. And that's pro-evolution! You ought to think real hard about that, Judge, before you go walking all over the Bible. It's your conscience, that's all I'm saying. The defense rests.

JUDGE EASTERBROOK: Thank you, Mr Crenshaw, for that stunning summation. This court sentences you to six months in the State Penitentiary of Tennessee. Good afternoon.

Some Place Better Than This

My Old Man's name was Jack Daniels Crenshaw. No surprise what he liked to drink. As a very small child I remember teething, cryin' out savagely for relief. Eventually he would appear over my crib and rub Jack Daniel's on his gums until he fell asleep.

Several years later, those very teeth fell out. When the first one went, my momma told me to put it under my pillow for the tooth fairy. That night, pretendin' to sleep, I felt her creep into the room and replace it with a quarter. Later I was awakened by my Old Man, hoverin' recklessly over the bed. He brusquely pulled the pillow aside, and pocketed my quarter.

'In this family,' he said, 'we don't sell off our body parts.'

He returned my tooth.

The Old Man's pride was his pompadour – a magnificent backswept pavilion of hair, Brylcreme slick, shiny and silvery as a nest of sardines. It was as intimidating as it was ridiculous. Charlie Rich would not have stayed in the same room with him. Conway Twitty would have backed down. My Old Man's hair defied gravity and created expectations the sonofabitch could never hope to live up to.

In the few grainy photos I've seen of him he's alone and wary, like a wolf. We never got into those pictures, my momma and me. Hell, we wasn't what you would call a real family, anyway. In fact, by the time I was old enough to carry a wallet, I never bothered to remove those fake pictures of relatives that came in the photo compartment. I'd pretend those people were my real family. 'That's my daddy,' I'd say to someone, pointin' to the photo. Sometimes they'd get suspicious and say, 'Wait a minute. I saw that guy when I bought a wallet.' I'd tell 'em my daddy was a professional 'Wallet Model'.

I spent my childhood starin' at him through bars, first from my crib, then later, prison, after he got sent up for tax fraud, sedition and poaching. My momma would take me to visit him. Through a square of greasy, smudged perspex he'd tell me he liked it in there. You got sheet cake for dessert every night, and you could shoot all the hoops you wanted. The reason for the barbed fences, the guards in the tower, he'd say, was to keep folks from *tryin' to get in*. Me, I believed him. Hell, I couldn't wait to get in there myself.

In prison he stamped out license plates that read *Tennessee: The Volunteer State*. I guess maybe that word, *volunteer*, got drummed into him, because when he got out, he'd found himself a new career – as a Human Guinea Pig and professional Lab Rat.

During his joint, he'd gotten paid fifty dollars to be 'voluntarily' injected with 'iron supplements'. The prison doctors told him it was for anemia research. But that ain't what it was at all. It was a federally sponsored study to determine if certain 'types' are genetically predisposed to criminal activity. My Old Man didn't give a flyin' fuck what it was for. Fifty dollars was fifty dollars. Around that same time, he learned his blood, Type O, was the premium blend hospitals paid good money for. By the time they'd released him from prison he decided he'd been put on this earth to be siphoned.

The same man who once told me we didn't sell our body parts now offered himself up like a three-dollar whore to every medical research project within drivin' distance. No one in the history of medicine was more of a medical pincushion than my Old Man. He got himself probed, prodded, sampled, drained, filtered, weighed, measured, shrunk, supplemented and fertilized beyond human limits. For twenty-five dollars he would cheerfully fill out any Stage 1 medical questionnaire. Fifty dollars got him naked and on a table. Throw him a C-note and he was yours to eviscerate as you pleased: MRI scans, EKGs, small-dosage radiation, sleep-deprivation studies, LSD testing, blood doping, skin grafts, fertility treatments. He'd have radioactive thymidine shot into his testicles (for steroid research) in the mornin', spend the entire afternoon at a tavern, then come home and try to bang my momma (or a neighbor), tellin' her he needed to monitor his sperm production. He absorbed Dow Chemical Dioxin as blithely as if it were Right Guard. He stayed bandaged, lumpy, swollen, stitched-up like an old saddle, slathered in experimental ointments, dubious creams, speculative unguents. Periodically, he sported an eyepatch that mysteriously kept shiftin' sides.

When he heard about the Tuskeegee Experiments, where black men down in Macon County, Alabama, were being injected with various strains of syphilis for seventy-five dollars (and funeral insurance vouchers), he stormed down there in his Bonneville and demanded to know why the offer wasn't open to a white man. In that respect, he was probably one of the earliest crusaders against reverse discrimination. He combed newspapers, hospitals, colleges and libraries for ads for research volunteers. He had a goddamned third-grade education but he knew what a double-blind placebo test was and exactly how much it paid. He wore snap-button Western shirts, not because of any cowboy ethic; they were just quicker to divest of in the exploratory ward.

The attendant nausea, rashes, dizziness, cramps, bloating, emaciation, bleeding gums, spade-shaped fingertips, weird breath, lack of depth perception, overnight breasts and other side effects that came with the job, he shrugged off. Not a single hair on his head faltered or fell out. The sonofabitch was indestructible. And every cent he made, he spent on Jack Daniel's.

Years later, though I suppose in some kind of direct sequence, I lost a tooth in a different way. My wife, Brenda #1, punched it out of me. Actually, she just loosened it enough to where I could pry it from my gums like a wet slippery watermelon seed.

'Thanks a lot,' was all I could think to say.

I never saw it comin'. Our marriage began and ended on a misunderstandin', which I blame on poor enunciation.

We'd been wed almost two years. In that previous sentence, the word 'wed' is in there twice, once as 'married' and once as a contraction of 'we had'. And that's as good an explanation for marriage as there is: 'We had.' *Marriage is the bucket that holds all the shit the two of you have been through together.*

Brenda #1, admired by all for her tireless charity work, was plannin' to run off with her ex-boyfriend as soon as he escaped from prison. I found that out because she was usin' my checkbook to finance it. And she'd stolen a car. It wasn't my car, but I was lookin' after it for someone and she just scarfed it, without so much as a how do you do.

She'd taken it up to Wartburg, Tennessee, right down the road from Brushy Mountain Correctional Facility. She was holed up at a motel, where, I reckon, she was tidyin' up minor details of springin' her asshole ex-boyfriend. And man, was he ever an asshole. That ain't just me sayin' that. Roughly two-thirds of America felt the same way on account of the fact that he was the guy who'd shot Dr Martin Luther King.

Knowin' that my wife's previous boyfriend was James Earl Ray had always been kind of a sore spot with me, particularly in light of the fact that she only started seein' him *after* he'd shot King. You might think it would be a subject we'd both dance around. I knew she was sensitive about it, especially since *he'd* dumped *her*. But it made me jealous.

When I say she'd been his girlfriend, I don't mean they dated or nothin' like that. He wasn't really in a position for courtship, seein' as how he was doin' ninety-nine years inside. But she visited him every chance she could, and they would shout their sweet nothin's at each other through the prison glass. What she saw in him, I'll never know. As far as I could tell, the man was an idiot, a total fuckin' bumbler. His first crime had been stealin' a wallet from a pair of men's pants hangin' in the window of a whorehouse in St Louis. He got chased down and roughed up by the owner of the pants. Imagine gettin' your ass kicked by someone in his jockeys. With a hard-on! That should be an indication maybe crime ain't your particular callin'. At Missouri State Penitentiary in Jefferson City, he tried to escape twice. The first time he fell and knocked himself out. The second time he got trapped in the prison's ceiling and couldn't find his way out. He finally gave himself up to the guards because he was hungry. The day he assassinated Dr King, he walked

11

out of a Memphis rooming house and dropped his rifle right on the pavement, where it was found, moments later, by the police. His fingerprints were all over it. This was the guy my wife used to call 'Sweetheart'.

So it was fairly temptin' to bring it up as much as I could. He made for a great scapegoat.

'I see you still ain't fixed that window in the bedroom,' she'd say. The window had come off its runners and kept rattlin' around when freight trains clattered by.

'You're right,' I'd answer. 'And you know what else I didn't do? . . . I DIDN'T KILL THE GREATEST LEADER THE CIVIL RIGHTS MOVEMENT HAS EVER HAD!!'

And that would pretty much settle her hash right there.

Truth of the matter is, I always kinda secretly thought I wasn't complicated enough for Brenda. Women like complex men, even if they tell you they don't. The more mercurial, the more they want to figure you out. Me, I'm shallow, and proud of it. Hell, people *drown* in the deep. Shallow, you got some place to put your feet. Women are drawn to complexity 'cause they've got about eight thousand different emotions and, what's more, an additional seventy-nine thousand quasi-hybrid-mutant *semi-emotions* that, as a man, you couldn't possibly hope to plumb. You can say, 'Are you angry?' and they'll answer, 'No, I'm betrayed and wistful. And limpid.' Shit like that. So you can lay a lot of complicated stuff on them and they're up for it. Women like a project!

James Earl Ray, inept as he was, must've intrigued Brenda. She was doin' volunteer work for the East Tennessee Eyeglass Bank and one day they asked her to go up to Brushy Mountain Correctional Facility to deliver a new pair of spectacles to him. She told me later, the moment she met him she'd seen somethin' in his eyes that made her believe he

12

never killed King. 'Cataracts,' I said, 'that's what you saw.' She felt he'd been set up. And the more she looked into the facts the more she became convinced he was a patsy. She started payin' visits to him at Brushy, bringin' him newspaper and magazine articles, toiletries and eyewear accessories. Next thing you know he was writin' letters to her and tellin' her he loved her, and she got mushy on him, even though the sonofabitch – and I can't emphasize this enough – HAD SINGLE-HANDEDLY TRIED TO NAIL THE COFFIN LID ON THE CIVIL RIGHTS MOVEMENT!! On top of that, he was almost fifty fuckin' years old.

I honestly don't know what she saw in him. I guess he made her feel wistful and limpid.

Then he betrayed her. Dumped her for a courtroom sketch artist named Anna who he'd been exchangin' little drawings of mountains and flowers with behind Brenda's back. Hell, if it weren't for Brenda givin' him those glasses, he wouldn't have even been able to find his paintbrush in the first place. One day she showed up to visit him and he told her he didn't want to have nothin' to do with her anymore. Then he got up and walked away from the visitors' glass. She sat there stunned. I saw the whole thing from the next window over. I'd come up to Brushy to visit my Old Man who was back inside for stealin' medical equipment.

I caught her on the rebound. We started goin' out and anyone woulda figured the whole James Earl Ray business was past her.

Two months later I proposed to her at the Pickle Barrel, my neighborhood sandwich shop. In the middle of the lunch rush, I said, 'Will you marry me?' I tried to time it between bites of her roast-beef sandwich, but the question caught her just as she dipped in.

'Who's William Aramy?' she said, munchin' loudly. She

13

looked annoyed. There was a dot of mustard on her nose.

Then, before I could repeat it, she jabbed at my hand.

'I need to tell you something.' She jerked her head, indicatin' the table behind us, a young couple with a little girl. The girl had palsy or multiple sclerosis, some kind of withering affliction, and was makin' gurgling noises.

'I cain't enjoy my food when there's a retard in the room,' she said, like it was somethin' she'd meant to tell me on our first date, but forgot.

'I know that ain't right, but it's just me. Anyway . . . William who?'

I didn't ask her again until we were in the parkin' lot, well clear of any retards.

Love, then Marriage, then Babies. That's the normal progression, ain't it? Unless you're White Trash, in which case it's usually Babies *then* Marriage. Love don't always figure into the equation.

The way I see it, everyone is about 3 percent real. That's the 3 percent of yourself that *no one* can ever get to. Most of us ain't even sure where it is inside us because it's been watered down by the other 97 percent: the part that's been sold. Sold to the boss, the bank, the finance company, friends, parents, enemies, everyone you ever knew. We all have the soul of a Lab Rat.

Eventually you reach the point where you actually *believe* you're this person you've sold yourself as. Then someone comes along who cuts through that bullshit – who sees right through you to your core. They've got your fuckin' number. So to protect yourself, you fall in Love with 'em to keep their mouth shut. Love is chloroform.

Brenda and me skipped the Babies and went straight to Marriage, figurin' Love wouldn't be too far behind.

Is that so crazy? To marry first, then hope it works out?

14

Ain't that how it works in lots of countries? I'd read some-where that in the Middle East, arranged marriages have a 3 percent failure rate. How is it that two people who hardly know each other get along better than couples who think they're soulmates hand delivered to each other by kismet? *'Cause they didn't let their hearts make stupid decisions for 'em!* Also, I understand someone loses a hand if it goes down the dumper. Don't quote me on that.

Something else I heard: in Saudi Arabia, to put paid to it, the husband just has to say 'I divorce thee' three times. The beauty of that is its simplicity; a slidin' scale of rapprochement. You could really use that to your advan-tage. 'I divorce thee . . . I divorce thee . . . I . . . make me a sandwich, now!'

Two years, we'd stayed together. Every time we went back to the Pickle Barrel, I'd remind her this is where it started.

'We're doin' alright, ain't we?' I'd say. The conviction there was paper thin.

'I don't follow.'

'I'm doin' my best to make you happy.'

'I get that part, but when do we go some place better than this?'

'I like this restaurant.'

'I didn't mean the restaurant.'

Brenda did her charity work. (Presumably, her altruism drew the line at dealin' with retards.) I fixed cars for Walt's German Auto Repair over on Euclid Avenue in South Knoxville.

Up till then, I'd had myself maybe two dozen different jobs and gotten shitcanned from every one. What I'd learned was, people don't lose their job 'cause they don't work hard enough, they lose their job 'cause they can't deal with other

15

people. And that was me. The less people I had to face, the less chance I had of gettin' fired. Because workin' with other human beings is stressful; workin' alone ain't, and that explains why it's always disgruntled postal workers who shoot up the workplace and never beekeepers. I spent all my time underneath a greasy automobile belly, and that was fine by me. I didn't have to look at the scrubbed, pampered, patronizing, milk-fed faces of the pompous assholes who brought in their Mercedes and BMWs. I wheeled around on a wooden creeper all day with my feet pokin' out from under a chassis and if you wanted to talk to me about your car, you addressed my shoes. My theory is, the closer you are to the ground, the less tension.

Still, it was a filthy, stinkin', thankless, no-hope job.

America is supposed to be the Land of Dreams. Well keep on dreamin'! That same tooth fairy who welshed on me as a kid has kept comin' back to steal every damn quarter I've ever got my bruised knuckles across. The Big Lie about America is that it's a classless society. Bullshit! In America, your name is a giveaway to where you stand on the ladder. If it's on the outside of the buildin' you work in, you're rich. If it's on a desk, you're middle class. And if it's on your shirt pocket, you're fuckin' poor. Bust your ass, reach high enough and you can dip into the cookie jar, same as anyone else. That's the word on the street. Scrub up nice and kiss ass and say 'yessir' and 'no sir', and one day that'll be *your* name on the outside of the buildin'.

Except it won't.

There's two colors in America: Green and Not-Green. When you're poor, the aggregate issue of black, white, Latino, Asian, Indian is just a monochrome rainbow against the bigger backdrop of who's Green and who ain't. 'Colored' and 'White' may have disappeared off of toilet doors but it was still printed clearly on the washin' machine at our neighborhood laundromat – the one we had to go to because I couldn't afford to buy my wife a washer/dryer combo. And I knew which button I had to push to get rid of all the stink, grease, sweat, dirt, lint, oil, gasoline, transmission fluid and blood that caked the shirt with my name on it.

'When do we go some place better than this?'

One day, I was goin' through the kitchen trash for some half-smoked cigarette butts and I found a Brushy Prison visitor's pass. Now why would she be goin' up there? All I could figure was she'd picked up with that ratface James Earl Ray again. I sat down at the kitchen table with a bottle of Old Grand-Dad bourbon and pictured them, starin' forlornly into each other's eyes through the prison glass, hands splayed against each other's like a couple of tree frogs. My whole brain turned to red mist.

She came home later that afternoon. I was still at the kitchen table.

'Did you go up to Brushy?' I said.

She didn't answer right away. She stood at the window, starin' out at the freight train tracks.

'Yeah.'

'Why?'

'Why do you think? To visit your daddy.'

'Oh. How's he doin'?'

'Same ol'.'

'I see.'

'You ain't been up there to see him since we married,' she said.

'I got nothin' to say to him.'

'Well, I figgered he might like some company.' She went over to the cupboards and flung the doors open, huntin' for dinner.

'I divorce thee . . . I divorce thee . . .' I was thinkin' to myself. My Old Man had been let out of Brushy eighteen months ago.

She made herself a sandwich.

The next day, Brenda stole a car, a 450 SLC Mercedes. The car was a road rocket, a collector's dream. All-aluminum engine, low, rakish and priceless. It was sittin' in a bay in Walt's garage, right by the overhead doors. She breezed in, grabbed the keys off the corkboard and drove off in it. I was underneath another car the whole time. All I saw was her ankles.

I knocked off early and drove home in my pickup, past the usual shops. Shops with windows full of stuff I couldn't buy for her. I couldn't understand why she would tear off in a car that wasn't hers. When I got home, I discovered her closet cleaned out. My checkbook was missin' as well. The instinct, right under my skin, was of things comin' unglued.

A week later some canceled checks showed up and it all got real crystal clear. There, in contemptuous handwritin', was my signature! Made out to the Holiday Inn in Wartburg, Tennessee. There were checks to a Texaco station. There were checks to a Waffle House and a coupla other restaurants. And – the kicker – a check for $176.54 to some place called Huntley's Men's Wear. Now why would a gal be buying menswear? For someone in a prison jumpsuit, that's what!

I knew then, I *just knew*, she was gonna run away with him! To Canada maybe, or south to Mexico or Central America, or wherever it is assassins mingle.

The canceled checks had arrived in an urgent lookin'

18

envelope along with an overdraft notice for $1412.87, and there was a note in there to call a certain Mr T. Grantham at the Bank of Knoxville to work out some kind of pay arrangement. *T*! The man wants to talk to me about *my* money and won't even tell me his first name? I bet this Mr T. Grantham, whoever he was, went home every day and said to his wife, 'Guess what, honey, *everybody* I talked to today called me an asshole!'

I always knew that checking account was gonna get me in trouble. It was the one and only time in my life I'd ever had one and the only reason I'd applied for it was because Brenda insisted. Alright, that ain't completely true. I wanted a checking account to feel like I was more than just trash – to feel like I had somethin' over my Old Man. So I applied for it, figurin' I'd be turned down. Next thing I know, a box of personalized checks shows up in the mail with creepy little pastel floral scenes all over 'em. I guess they'd approved me because, for the first time, I finally had a steady job.

I called up the number on the bank letter and asked to speak to Mr T. Grantham. I wondered if my movements were represented by pinheads on a map. Right now this T. Grantham fella was probably whisperin', 'We got him!', his hand mufflin' the phone, while around him, the Operation Crenshaw team scrambled.

He came on the line.

'Good afternoon, Mr Crenshaw?'

'Yeah.'

'How are you?'

'I was told to call this number.'

'Yes. You've been referred to our department [Aha!] due to your, uh, somewhat extravagant expenditures of late.'

'It was my wife. She ran off with my checks.'

'I see. Is she there?'

'How can she be here? I just said she ran off, didn't I?'

'Did she make the purchases without your authorization?'

'Somethin' like that, yeah.'

'Well, you realize, as her spouse, you are still responsible for the overdraft.'

'But I didn't make the purchases.'

'It doesn't matter.'

'It matters to me. It's my damn checks.'

'You say she "ran off". To where?'

'She ran off to do some volunteer prison work.'

'That's tax deductible you know.'

'I don't pay taxes!'

'That's interesting.'

'And I ain't gonna pay for somethin' I didn't buy! Find my wife. Get the money from her.'

There was a long pause.

'I wouldn't try to use that checkbook again if I was you, Mr Crenshaw.'

'How can I use it if I don't have it?'

The Mercedes' owner came around lookin' for his car. Walt, my boss, stalled him. He said the car was at a body shop right now, waitin' for special paint to arrive from Stuttgart. Walt was a decent old coot with a set of teeth far too large and white for his mouth. I always suspected they were factory-made and someone had got the orders mixed up. Car owners saw precision in those choppers and trusted Walt with their vehicle.

'I want the car back, friend,' the owner said to Walt.

'I ain't your friend,' Walt answered. But you could tell he didn't like friction with the public. He'd been in the same location for twenty-five years.

When the owner left, Walt flexed his teeth at me. 'You better get that crazy little Bathsheba of yours in line,' he warned, ''cause right now, you ain't worth shit.'

'I will,' I said.

I got in my old pickup and headed over to Farragut, turned North on 62, past Oak Ridge, and headed up to Wartburg.

How come, you might ask, if my wife had stolen a car, run off with my checkbook, and planned to spring a world-caliber assassin, didn't I call the police?

Here's why. Even though she was a bleedin' heart, myopic, Stockholm-syndromed, right-wing, conspiracy nutcake with fantastic tits, she was my wife. And I ain't, nor will I ever be, a snitch.

It wasn't my deal, this James Earl Ray business. Brenda used to go on and on about it. She'd pull out her flow charts – weird, parabolic diagrams of overlapping conspiracies. Why was there never a public trial? 'Cause it would have turned into a never-endin' hunt, a domino chase, she'd argue. The FBI was in on it. Everyone knew J. Edgar Hoover had a hard-on for Martin Luther King. The CIA was likely involved. They didn't like him comin' out against Vietnam. There were rural-type black leaders who didn't cotton to his non-violent themes. There was someone in Montreal named Raoul who may or may not have been James Earl Ray's brother, Jerry Ray, who was a compatriot of J. B. Stoner, the crooked lawyer who also headed the National States Rights Party when he wasn't busy bombin' black churches. There was a St Louis Mafia connection. Various nests of Ku Klux Klansmen festering in the shadows, white supremacist police cabals, influential Southern businessmen, so on and so on. One thing was for certain: the stupid oaf wasn't capable of pullin' off the assassination by his lonesome. So it

21

stood to reason there was more to this prison escape than my wife's wistful leanings for a wronged patsy. She had to be mixed up with some pretty nasty characters. The less I knew, the better. Like I said earlier, the fewer assholes I had to deal with in life, the better. I was just a simple mechanic, tryin' to hold on to my job.

All I wanted was the stolen car back. And my checks. And my wife.

I got to Wartburg and it looked just like I expected: a town with a prison breathin' down its neck. You had to wonder who talked these people into putting it there: *'Folks, we're gonna round up the state's grisliest murderers, rapists, pedophiles and drug addicts and put 'em right here in your town. And that means jobs, jobs, jobs!! Who's with me?'*

I found the Holiday Inn, grazed through the parkin' lot twice and saw no sign of the Mercedes. I parked and went inside and asked at the desk if an Otis Lee Crenshaw was registered.

The desk clerk pulled a list from under the register, shielding it from me with what I felt to be unnecessary secrecy.

'Yeah. "Otis Lee Crenshaw". She's been here a while.'

'Doesn't "Otis" strike you as an unusual name for a woman?'

'What's that supposed to mean?'

'It means, *I*'m Otis Lee Crenshaw.'

He looked around, maybe wishin' he wasn't the night manager. In the daytime you got businessmen, families in station wagons, Kiwanis Club luncheoners and no riff-raff whatsoever.

'My wife signed *my* name to a check,' I tried to explain to him. 'I guess that slipped right by you.'

He decided to start over again.

'How can I help you, sir?'

22

'I'd like the key to my room.'

'What room is that?'

'The one registered to Otis Lee Crenshaw.'

He rechecked the register, then handed me a key.

'You're an idiot,' I said.

On my way through the lobby he called after me, 'They screen for this job, y'know. The bad seeds get weeded out fast!'

Brenda wasn't in the room. I looked around for my check-book and couldn't find it. I went back downstairs and asked the desk clerk for a copy of all the phone calls from my room. He was startin' to act irritated.

'You just got here, didn't you?'

'No, I've been here for a week. Dressed as a woman. Gimme the fuckin' phone charges.'

She'd made quite a few calls. St Louis, Missouri. Columbus, Georgia. Piedras Negras, Mexico. Dozens of other places as well. I could've dialed any of those numbers and asked what was goin' on with Brenda. But I just didn't wanna' know. 'Cause then I'd be in on it – a real donkey ride to hell.

I went back up to the room and laid down on the bed and thought, 'This don't seem right'. It wasn't my room, but I recognized all the stuff in it. Her suitcase, her bag of curlers, her brand of shampoo, her bras, her skirts, her tops scattered everywhere. I felt like a familial intruder. For some strange reason, that gave me an erection.

Then I heard footsteps in the hall, a click of the door lock.

She didn't even look surprised to see me. Maybe the desk clerk had mentioned somethin' to her.

'Whaddya know?' she said. 'It's you. I'm goin' to have a bath. If you're nice you can join me.'

She was wearin' a tight, pale skirt and tomato-colored

blouse. She began undoin' the buttons, baring her tanned neckline. She seemed to be treatin' this as some kind of sly seduction.

'What's goin' on?' I said.

'What do you mean?'

'I need to know where we're headed with all this.'

'To the tub.' She laughed loudly, flingin' her blouse over a chair. 'Run it, will you? Hot.' She pulled some bobby pins out of her hair, put them in her teeth, went over to the mirror and shook her hair loose.

I went into the bathroom and turned on the taps. Then she came in, naked.

'Whatever you're gonna say, you won't get it right,' she said. 'Do I look drunk? I'm tiddly.'

She leaned on the sink. I was thinkin', 'I really need to take control here,' but I was confused and my erection was cancelin' everything out. I took off my clothes and climbed in the tub, then she climbed in and we both just sat there. I stared down at the half of me underwater. I looked like some weird sea creature.

I wanted to ask her, point blank, if she was about to spring James Earl Ray. But if I brought it up, there would be no turnin' back. It would be my deal. So instead I just said, 'I was thinkin' we should move away. Maybe some place like Florida.'

'I'll tell you what, Otis, I like it pretty well in this motel room.'

'I think you're gettin' yourself into somethin' a lot deeper than you imagine.'

'If it's all too much for you, you need to stay outta my way.'

'I ain't gotta listen to this,' I shot back.

'The trouble with you is you have no understanding of the people who have been fucked over in this world.'

24

She stood up and climbed out of the tub, leaving me with my hard-on pokin' up like a periscope.

'I've left you,' she said, 'because, what I know now is, you're never gonna punch above your weight.'

There was nothin' I could say. I sat there, feelin' I was on the cusp of some sinister vortex where Klansmen, St Louis Mafia types, guys named Raoul, shadowy underworld specters, giant domino slabs, were all ready to slam down on me just for askin' the wrong question – any question. Christ, they could've been in the next room! Maybe James Earl Ray was already out. Maybe he was in the ceiling right above our heads. I couldn't ask her a damned thing. I might as well have been chloroformed.

I went back to Knoxville with my checkbook. No Mercedes. No Brenda. One out of three.

I came home to my empty house and sat there drinkin' Old Grand-Dad and tryin' to figure just what to do next. I missed my wife. But the woman in that motel room wasn't the Brenda I'd married. That woman was a trainwreck ghost.

The phone would ring and I'd answer it, hopin' it was her, but it was always T. Grantham. His calls were gettin' more and more terse.

'You need to steer yourself right down here and sort this out, Mr Crenshaw.'

'I ain't gonna sort nothin' out. It's not my deal.'

'We have a little thing we call accrued interest.'

'That's nice for you.'

'You can monkey around, Mr Crenshaw. But the Bank of Knoxville will see to a deadbeat like you.'

Two days later, James Earl Ray escaped with six other inmates. It was all over the news. I sat in front of the television and watched the hoopla. The Morgan County Sheriff came on and said they'd have no trouble findin' him.

'If the FBI stay outta my way,' he said, eerily.

The FBI came on and said James Earl Ray had three hundred dollars and was headed to South America. The Sheriff said no he wasn't. He was right under their noses and his little honeymoon was goin' to be over real shortly. *Honeymoon*? What did that mean? But no one mentioned Brenda. Or a Mercedes.

The FBI and the local police were steppin' all over each other's dicks. Anyone watchin' the TV could tell that. The followin' day, there was still no sign of James Earl Ray. Someone reported gunshots in the woods above the prison. It turned out two county deputies had fired at a black FBI agent. The FBI chief said the deputies were tryin' to kill the black agent. One of the deputies came on and explained that was entirely not the case.

'If we'd wanted to kill him, we wouldn't of aimed over his head,' the deputy said. He had a look of insouciance on his face, as if this whole thing was just your regular Saturday Night Fish-fry.

I sat there for two days, waitin' for Brenda's picture to come up on the screen.

The phone rang and it was T. Grantham. He didn't seem interested in talkin' about the escape.

'You carcass. Pay up,' he seethed, then hung up.

Fifty-four hours after James Earl Ray escaped, they found him. He was up in the woods above Brushy, hidin' under a pile of leaves. A pair of deputies had heard bloodhounds howlin'. When the deputies got there, the dogs were lickin' James Earl Ray's feet.

Up in the woods. There was only one way in and out of Brushy and that was down the road to Wartburg. All he had to do was go down that road and the whole world would have opened up. But no, the idiot goes up in the woods.

I pictured Brenda, sittin' at the end of the road in the stolen car, waitin' for him. It seemed sad. Your choice is a getaway with a beautiful gal, or a pile of wet leaves, and you settle for the leaves. That right there, my friend, is hard-core Dumpsville.

She came back. Dropped the Mercedes' keys on the table and stood there tremblin'.

'I'm sorry,' she said, as if that would kick the knife under the table.

She went into the bathroom and started the shower. This time, I wasn't invited. I waited until the water stopped runnin' and walked in.

'I divorce thee . . .' I said.

She was dryin' herself off furiously, her back to me.

'You divorce *the* what?'

'I divorce thee . . .'

She turned and looked at me quizzically.

'*The* . . . what? What are you talking about?'

'Thee. I divorce thee.'

There, that was it. Done.

'I'm just not followin' you.'

'Yes you are. I've divorced you.'

Then she punched me in the mouth.

I fished a loose tooth from my gums and spat blood into the tub. 'Thanks a lot,' I said. I wasn't even angry. I reckon she was too young and too frustrated by life and marriage, thinkin' the entire range of men ran from James Earl Ray to me and back again, and hell, I just felt sorry for her.

*   *   *

27

T. Grantham called.

'How does it feel to be you?' I said.

'Beg pardon?'

'You. How does it feel to imprison people every day? 'Cause that's what debt is, ain't it? Prison. Does it make you feel powerful?'

'Powerful?'

'Restrictin' people's movements. Puttin' the screws to 'em. Tell you what. You win. You got me. You're the big boss man.'

I hung up. Then I dialed him back.

'Permission to take a piss, Big Boss Man Grantham?' I sang out, as soon as he came on the line. Then, I hung up again. For the next week or so, I called him up every twenty minutes to ask Big Boss Man's permission. Permission to put on my shoes. Permission to eat. Permission to go out in the yard. Permission to change the TV channel.

T. Grantham stopped takin' my calls. So I drove down to the bank and stood in the middle of the lobby, unbuttonin' my shirt and yellin', in a lyrical prison workfarm cadence, 'Takin' it off today, Big Boss Bank! Been draggin' the line double time!'

Pretty soon I was half naked, whippin' my shirt around like a lariat and yellin', 'Rippety-tippety-ti-yi-yay!!'

T. Grantham came out of his office and ordered the security guard to restrain me. Then he locked all the employees inside the bank.

'*Now* who's the prisoner?' I yelled, lyin' on the floor.

Drinking to Forget

I got over Brenda the only way I know how. I drank myself through the heartbreak. Now there's a right way and a wrong way to go about that. Examine the lyrics of these two songs:

> He's a candidate for detox
> A graduate from the school of hard knocks
> Since she changed the locks
> And kicked him out again
> He puts a quarter in the jukebox
> Orders another whiskey on the rocks
> Then turns around and coldcocks
> The fella beside him
> He's got a drinkin' problem
> Since she said goodbye
> He's got a drinkin' problem
>
> > > Boyd Banks and the
> > > Earthrods, 'Drinkin'
> > > Problem'

> I got a pickup truck and a big ol' bag of quarters
> I know every jukebox bar from here to Maine

29

I'm gonna be so drunk by the time I reach the border
I won't be able to recall her name
Then I'll drink Canada Dry
I'll drink Canada Dry
I won't think of her at all
From Winnipeg to Montreal
Cause tonight I'm drinkin' Canada dry

Buddy Ray Wirtz,
'Drinking Canada Dry'

These, of course, are examples of Drinking to Forget, a recurrent theme in literally thousands of crappy country songs. (Actually, if you really study them, they're Drinking to Remember songs, since both main characters appear to be usin' alcohol to revive their memories instead of kill them.) Still, the scenario is familiar: some sad bastard commandeers the jukebox while attemptin' to drink his (her) way through a heartbreak. In other words, a public display of a very private matter.

Your broken heart is your own business and draggin' other bar patrons into your quagmire of despair is *wrong, fuckin' wrong*. They're tryin' to have a good time, for cryin' out loud! Maybe they'd like to hear a little upbeat music on the jukebox, but no, Johnny Dumppants has shown up with a mountain of quarters to play the same goddamn dirge over and over and everyone in hearin' distance has to stew in his despair.

If musicians and distillers have one thing in common it's this: they know there's money in Heartbreak. Accordin' to the US Wine, Beer and Spirits Association, four cents of every dollar spent on alcoholic beverages is from someone Drinking to Forget.* But that don't mean bartenders

---

*Alright, I just made that up. But it's probably true.

want them as patrons! The Drinking-to-Forget drinker actually drives other drinkers away. They flee to another bar. Thus, the cumulative financial largesse of Drinking to Forget seldom benefits the individual bar owner.

Likewise, the artist who records this kind of song is cynically exploitin' the heartbreak victim. He knows he's gonna earn about seven cents every time one of his weepfests gets played on the jukebox. Both of the songs above have earned hundreds of thousands of dollars for their respective performers. However, I'm willin' to bet only a handful of people ever *heard* them. They just got played over and over by the same lovelorn sap about a million times.

Goin' into the same bar night after night and pickin' at old sores ain't the way to get over a broken heart. You're just draggin' out a pain that should have healed a long time ago. In other words, if you're gonna Drink to Forget, stay the hell at home!

Keep this in mind: the heart is a muscle, not a bone. You can't break a muscle, you can only sprain it. And the repetitive motion of pinin' at bars and punchin' jukeboxes only aggravates the situation.

The best way to get over your 'broken' heart is to experience some true pain: somethin' that puts a strained muscle into proper perspective. Go to the hardware store and get yourself one of those six-foot wooden paint ladders. Take a big marker pen and on the bottom rung, write ALONE. Then on the next step, write ATTRACTION. On the next, SEX. On the step next to the top, write ROMANCE. Then, on that rickety fold-out platform where the paint can goes, the one that reads THIS IS NOT A STEP!, write LOVE.

Now, start climbin' the ladder. Notice how each rung gets a little more excitin' and precarious? Now, step on to the LOVE platform and . . . whoopsedaisy, there . . .

CRUNCH!!! . . . . watch your sorry ass come tumblin' all the way down, dribblin' your chin on every rung until you're back at ALONE. Now what you're experiencin' is *true pain*, possibly even a spinal injury. How does that compare to your achy breaky little heart? Remember, there's only one kind of heartbreak, but there's a million kinds of hurt.

Country Radio

You had to wonder what was gonna become of Wayne Pennegar. The day he got doubled up with me the guards dragged him over from C Wing and threw his belongings on the bunk below mine. He had bruises all over his face and a patch of hair missin' from his scalp. No one had told me I was gonna get a cellmate and I sure as hell wasn't too thrilled about it.

'Sit someplace where I can't see you,' I said to him.

The cell was eight by twelve.

Eventually it became impossible to ignore the fact that I was stuck with a cellmate. Wayne claimed to be in a biker gang called the Satan Chasers. I didn't believe him and told him he looked too damn stringy to even hold up a Sportster if it tipped over.

'Well think again,' he said, and pulled out a photo from his pile of belongings. He waggled it at me.

'What is it?' I asked.

'That's my initiation,' he said.

It showed a greasy, tattooed biker in a green surgical mask. The biker was holdin' a naked Barbie doll delicately in his fingers. He was poised to slap it, like he'd just delivered it from a womb. At the bottom of the photo, blurry, but unmistakable, was a man's protruding ass. I guessed that would be Wayne. I handed the photo back to him.

'I'd keep that photo to myself,' I advised him.

'But it's the Satan Chasers,' he said.

'Suit yourself. I think you might put the wrong idea into some heads around here.'

'I can handle myself,' he said.

From the looks of him, I wasn't so sure. He'd been worked over pretty good. I didn't ask where the bruises came from. I knew sooner or later he'd tell me.

By the followin' day, everyone knew. He'd been jumped by a couple of Tennessee Stompers, a rival biker gang who ran C Wing.

I'd been sentenced to six months at Turney Work Farm for attempted kidnapping. Turney was up in Only, Tennessee. The word was it wasn't too bad, that I could've done worse.

But I was skeptical 'cause I'd never heard Turney mentioned in any songs, and I'd been hopin' to be sent somewhere musically glorified, like Nashville Prison – the setting for '(I Washed My Hands) In Muddy Water' by Hank Snow.

Turney called itself 'progressive'. There was a seventy-five-acre tomato farm and you could take courses in arc welding, sheet metal or makin' box springs for mattresses. You could have a radio in your cell, a tiny one, generously provided by the State of Tennessee. The radio sat on a shelf above the wash basin. It looked like a toy. I kept the dial on WSN out of Nashville: the best country music station in the South.

I'd grown up on Hank Williams, Patsy Cline, George Jones, Jim Reeves: plaintive music that trailed from the radio like smoky cotton, which is how it was meant to sound, high and lonesome. Doleful singers wailin' about heartache, hard work, prison, bein' broke or drunk or torn up inside. The little green prison radio, with its anemic speaker, suited that kind of sound just fine.

One afternoon, out of the blue, Wayne went over and switched it to another station. I couldn't believe his unmitigated gall. He frapped around the dial until he found some kind of raucous redneck squawl – Foghat or Lynyrd Skynyrd or Black Oak Arkansas maybe. It was hard to tell because, from the pathetic radio, the song just sounded strangled.

'I can't take no more of your hick music,' he said, and started drummin' on his mattress.

I went over to the radio and switched it back to WSN.

'You need to un'erstand me right here and now,' I said. Then I told him a little somethin' about hick music. Johnny Paycheck shoots a man in the head over an argument about how to prepare turtle soup. Ernest Tubb pulls out his .357 Magnum and blasts the lobby of an insurance buildin'. Charlie Rich, disgusted at havin' to announce John Denver as the winner at some music awards show, sets the winner's card on fire and calls him a *pussy*. Faron Young dives offstage and from the audience grabs a six-year-old girl who's been stickin' her tongue out at him, and spanks her.

'That ain't your cheap rock and roll posturing,' I said. 'Country music walks the talk.'

'Six years old, hunh?' said Wayne, suddenly interested.

We're sittin' in the half-dark cell, smokin' and talkin' bullshit. The radio is playin' a Dottie West song, 'Let Me Off At The Corner'.

I tell Wayne that Dottie West posed naked for *Oui* magazine at the age of fifty. I'd seen the spread and she didn't look half bad, neither.

'How many naked women you seen, Otis?' he asks.

35

'In the flesh? My share.'

'Not me.'

'What?'

'I never seen a naked gal.'

'But you're a Satan Chaser. What do you fellas do all day, knit?'

'You must've had a lotta tail, hunh, Otis? I know you have. Tell me about one time.' He says it like Lennie askin' George about the rabbits in *Of Mice and Men*.

This conversation is makin' me uncomfortable. It's best in prison not to get too wistful about the way things were before.

'I don't really wanna talk about it.'

'I wish't I was better lookin',' Wayne says.

'Better lookin' and smarter', I think to myself. I'd seen his tattoo, a skeleton with a cocktail glass. Underneath the skeleton were the words 'Satin Chasers'.

Not long after that, an inmate named Charles Pillow choked on a piece of pork in the dining hall. One minute he'd been talkin' about turkey huntin' and the next he was on the floor, huggin' the chair legs, bug-eyed and crimson. A guard raced across the room and got him in a bear hug. For a second, it looked like professional wrestlin'. The guard pumped him like a mustard squirt bottle and the pork shot out of his throat makin' a perfect arc across two dining tables. A few minutes later, Charles was back to his turkey story.

Any time cons can make life more difficult for the screws and administrators, they will. Charles went in to see the warden and complained the food servers nearly killed him.

'They're not cuttin' up the meat into small enough portions,' he said. He asked to file a form 1127, a prisoner abuse complaint. He knew all 1127s had to be investigated by the State Prisons' Board. That would gum up the works and create grief for the warden.

'You choked, Pillow,' the warden said. 'You were runnin' your mouth and forgot there was food in it.'

'I want the 1127,' Pillow said. 'And, I'll tell you what else. There ought to be some proper life-savin' trainin' in this unit. If that guard hadn't got to me, I'd be dead now.'

The warden said he would take that into consideration. He was, after all, open to new avenues of 'progressiveness'.

A few nights later, there was another chokin' incident. This time it was Wayne Pennegar. He was off by himself in a far corner and only after he'd climbed on to the table, gasping, did anyone notice. The same guard who'd saved Charles Pillow had to run over and give him a bear hug. Wayne was a lot scrawnier and the guard almost cracked his ribs. After that, the warden announced the prisoners would learn the Heimlich maneuver, the life-saving technique for chokin' victims.

So, one night after dinner, a group of us were marched over to the clinical ward. Someone had set out rows of chairs like a town meetin'. The assembly was supposed to be mandatory for all medium-level inmates and there were maybe thirty of us. There was a lot of grumblin' about this cuttin' into our rec time, and I saw Charles Pillow walk in, lookin' sheepish, like this was all his fault. The room shaped itself into ordained segregations. The old-timers sat to one side. The Tennessee Stompers had their own little cluster. The Cherokees huddled near the back, and the blacks fanned out across the front row, each with a seat between them. Several of the blacks wore shower caps to protect their hair activator. I looked around and saw Wayne Pennegar over in a corner by himself.

Presently, a man in a rumpled dark suit came into the

room. He wore thick-rimmed glasses, a small Texas Ranger-style Stetson and had a black bushy beard that encircled his mouth like a toilet brush. He had a life-saving dummy in his arms, which he laid on a table behind him.

The man said his name was Curtis Pill and he was somethin' or other from Tulane University down in New Orleans. When he pronounced his name, most of us thought he'd said 'coitus pill'. His Cajun accent was as impenetrable as molasses and through the entire demonstration we barely understood a word he said. For example, he kept sayin' 'eesofaggus' until it finally dawned on us he was talkin' about the esophagus. He called the trachea the 'truckeea'. He was enormously entertaining.

'Dayus two kinda peeple in da woild,' he explained. 'Dose dat haff choked, and dose dat's gonna choke.' He made dramatic movements with his hands that made us all realize how close to kickin' it Charles Pillow had come. 'Turty seconds. Das all it takes for brain damage to set in. His fingernails is gonna toin blue. Mebbe he got dentures dat's fallin' back into his troat – dese are tings you got ta' be awayer of.'

By now, some of the men were pretendin' to choke, rollin' around on the floor. The whole thing was turnin' into a big hoot. I felt a little sorry for Curtis Pill. He was just tryin' to do his job. The black guys in their shower caps didn't quite know what to make of Curtis. They thought, with that accent of his, he was takin' the mickey. One of the blacks laughed in a way that sounded like he wasn't amused.

'Cracker motherfucker,' he muttered, loud enough for Curtis to hear.

Suddenly, Curtis Pill picked up the dummy and hurled it at the black guy. It hit the floor with a dull thud, skidded and came to a stop against his shoes.

'The co-wreck and proper pro-ceedure in dis instant,' Pill

calmly explained, 'is the Himelick manoober.' He stared straight at the black guy. 'Now who wants to volunteer to demonstrate dis pro-ceed-ure?'

The black guy stood up slowly. But he didn't volunteer. Instead, he kicked the dummy across the room where it floundered against a wall. Now it got really quiet. We were all waitin' to see what Curtis Pill was gonna do.

Then Wayne Pennegar sprang from his chair and went straight for the dummy, diving on it, like he was savin' a child from an oncomin' truck. He came up to a sittin' position, cradlin' the dummy. He stared down the black dude, givin' him the evil eye. Half the guys in the room were up out of their seats waitin' for somethin' to kick off. I was thinkin' I didn't wanna be there anymore.

Then, as we all watched in amazement, Wayne Pennegar began spankin' the Heimlich dummy on its ass.

'Don't . . . you . . . ever . . . stick . . . your . . . tongue . . . out . . . at . . . me!' he scolded it, in no uncertain terms. Then he crawled on top of the thing and started humping it. The guards were on him in no time.

It's lockdown: 10:30 p.m. Wayne is on his bunk. I'm sittin' on the floor of my cell smokin' Marlboros and listenin' to WSN's Saturday Night Swing Show: Bob Wills, Johnny Gimble, The Swift Jewel Cowboys, Patsy Montana and the Prairie Ramblers. One great tune after another.

The announcer does his own ads in between the songs, readin' 'em off cue cards or a script in a voice that modulates like a gentle roller coaster. He talks about Martha White Flour, how it makes perfect biscuits every time. 'It's self risin'!' he says and leaves it at that. He should've added, 'Just like Jesus!' Then he reads an ad for Gold Bond Medicated Powder, how it 'goes to work' on diaper rash, athlete's foot, bee stings, 'even . . . jock itch'. You can tell in his voice he was savorin' the naughty reference to jock itch. Then he introduces a Spade Cooley tune.

When the song comes on, I fill Wayne Pennegar in on Spade Cooley's rough and rowdy past. I tell him that it was Spade, not Bob Wills, who invented Western Swing back in the forties. He had a popular television show for a few years until he got unceremoniously dumped for an accordion player named Lawrence Welk. Spade never really got over bein' shitcanned for a twerp from North Dakota who played cornball champagne music for an audience of blue-haired ladies with bingo wings. One night in 1961, he stumbled home drunk to his house in Mojave, California, and kicked his wife to death while his fourteen-year-old daughter watched.

Spade aged fast in prison. He did nine years at Vacaville, up in Central California, and one day they let him out to go perform for a sheriff's benefit in Oakland. He walked out on stage, swung his fiddle to his chin and tore the roof off the place. He hadn't lost any of his jump in prison. Then he walked backstage and dropped dead.

I say to Wayne, 'What badass rockstar ever matched that?'

Wayne takes all this in like a child bein' told a bedtime story. Hell, he *looks* childlike, lyin' there on his bunk with the Heimlich dummy nestled in his arms. He's drawn bright red lips on it, and eyes with fluttery lashes, and he's given it a head of hair made from a prison floor mop. God knows how he'd got hold of it. Later, when I inspect the thing close up, I see holes poked into it in the relevant locations.

A few nights later, for no reason anyone could figure, Wayne jumped on to the dinin' table and waved his genitals in the air.

40

'I got jock itch to beat the band!' he announced. The guards spirited him off to his cell.

By now, all the other cons knew Wayne was a loony. They'd pass by the cell and see him lyin' there with his girlfriend.

'I am the leading fornicator in the Great State of Tennessee!' he would bellow. 'And you can all kiss my Dixie white ass!'

The cons would shake their heads and keep walkin'.

When the screws were around, he kept the dummy hid under his bunk, behind a stack of biker mags.

I went to the warden and told him I wanted to transfer cells. I didn't tell him Wayne Pennegar was a crazy misguided impressionable pervert who was, probably even as we were talkin', fuckin' a Heimlich dummy. Like I've always said, I ain't no snitch. I just told the warden I thought Wayne was trouble waitin' to happen. Those Tennessee Stompers were gonna get to him again and I didn't need that kind of shit in my cell. I was just tryin' to do my six months and get out.

The warden told me Turney wasn't a country club and I didn't have any choice in who I shared a cell with.

The screws came to my cell a few days later. I figured they'd heard about Wayne's dummy. Now it would be all over for him. They would put him on The Numbers. The Numbers is rule forty-three: Anyone found guilty of a sexual offense gets segregated for his own protection. It meant you got your own cell. But it also meant that every other con assumed the reason you were segregated was because you were a kiddy fiddler.

But the guards didn't come into the cell. They told me I had a visitor and led me down to Prison Reception. I reckoned it was Brenda. I didn't know what I was gonna say to her. She would want to talk about the divorce. As far as I was concerned, we were done, paperwork or no paperwork. But when I got to the glass, it was my Old Man.

'Well, ain't this somethin',' he cackled. 'I never thought I'd see the day I was sittin' on *this* side.'

'How are you?' I said.

'You're lookin' at it. I bought you some lottery tickets.' He fanned a stack of tickets at me, his idea of a father–son gesture.

'They said I should leave 'em with the guards.'

'Yeah. Thanks.'

'Any of these pay out, I get half.'

'Yeah. Sure,' I said. Now I was really wishin' it had been Brenda. I looked up and down the glass. Other men were talkin' to their gals. One chair over from my Old Man, a dark gal with a long chestnut braid down her back was talkin' to a con I'd never seen. Her eyes showed astonishment at everything he was sayin' to her. It must be somethin' to have a gal like that, I thought, one who doesn't miss a trick. She was the sexiest thing I'd ever seen and I barely heard my Old Man when he told me Momma had left him.

'It was Rudy,' the Old Man said.

'Who's Rudy?'

'Rudy, my barber,' he said. 'Your momma left me for a goddamned sheepshearer.'

'Now what?'

'I don't know. He's been lookin' after my hair for twenty years. I can't just cut him loose.'

'I don't mean the barber. You.'

'Me?'

'What are you gonna do with yourself?'

'I'll be fine. I got irons in the fire. No siree, you ain't got worry about ol' J.D. here.'

42

'You ought to get yourself another girlfriend,' I said. I knew my momma was better off without this sonofabitch.

'You can't rope the wind!' my Old Man barked, loud enough to turn the heads of most visitors.

'I was listenin' to the radio on the drive up here . . .' he said.

'Still drivin' the Bonneville?'

'Yepper,' he grunted, '. . . And Dean Martin comes on. He's singin' 'You're Nobody Till Somebody Loves You'. You've heard it?'

'I have.'

'Well, I stop the car right there and I talk to the radio. I say, "Wait a minute, Deano, are you sayin' everything I've done in my life is a complete waste . . . just because nobody loves me? Well, think again! Maybe I'm no big-time show-biz rat pack guy like you, but I am *somebody*. With or without love. You, Mr Martin, will not undermine *my* self worth!" You ever seen them Matt Helm flicks he does?'

'No.'

'Well, he's just cakewalkin' through 'em, you ask me.'

I watched the good-lookin' gal kiss her man through the perspex and get up to leave. She was cryin'. It broke my heart.

'That's the one thing in here they can't take from you,' my Old Man said, 'your self-worth. Remember that.'

'I will,' I replied.

'That's from me to you.'

Lockdown again.

The radio is on the Grand Ol' Opry. Even through the tiny speaker you can tell the house band is hot as a two-dollar pistol, tearin' through an old Merle Watson bluegrass number.

'What's his story?' says Wayne. Wayne thinks every country musician has a hard-luck story now and he's close to right. I tell him Wayne Merle's been dead a year or so.

'One of the greatest flat pickers ever.'

He asks me what that is.

'Playin' guitar with a pick on almost every finger.'

Like a lot of musicians, Merle was a night owl. And he enjoyed a little late-night open-top cruisin'. But his Speedster of choice was a tractor (the same as George Jones, who drove all over Nashville on a John Deere after his license had been revoked for drunk-drivin').

Anyway, one night Merle was doin' what any musical hellion would be at 2 a.m. – paneling his basement. He got a splinter stuck in his arm and decided to visit a neighbor to help him remove it. I reckon it must've been a balmy North Carolina night, because Merle opted to travel to the neighbor's by tractor. The neighbor 'anaesthetized' Merle with a coupla bottles of wine and removed the splinter. Merle headed back home. But he never made it. That tractor went over an embankment and pinned Merle beneath it, face down in his beloved bluegrass.

'No shit,' says Wayne from his bunk. His Heimlich girlfriend is nestled in his arm. The two of 'em look real happy.

'So if the highway to heaven is full of rockstars who drove too fast . . .' I say, 'at least Merle's on that tractor, makin' sure they can't get by.'

In the daytime we work the tomato patch. There's three guards who patrol the thirty of us, languidly pacing up and down the tomato rows with riot guns crooked in their elbows. Occasionally they shout out, to no one in particular: 'Everyone healthy? We gonna' knock it for a loop today!'.

We all have to use handtools to work the field. There's only one tractor, a green John Deere with a power rake

44

hooked up to the PTO. It sits empty in the noonday heat. Past the tomato fields is a big hurricane fence with concertina wire and, beyond that, jackrabbits and Tennessee fescue and the buildings of Only off in the distance, shimmering in heat.

We have to pull tomatoes off the vine and pile them into wooden crates. When the crates are full, we carry them over to an old red International Harvester stake bed truck with wooden sides. There's a water cooler there and, once you've dropped off a crate of tomatoes, you can get a drink of water.

My back is ablaze and sore from stoopin' for tomatoes, and the acidic pung that comes off the plants burns my nostrils and makes my skin itch. Four more months of this shit and I'm out.

I'm daydreamin' of every little thing I ever took for granted on the outside: gettin' in my truck and drivin' up to the White Hen Pantry for a six-pack; goin' to bed when I feel like it and gettin' up when I want to; the whine of semis rollin' down the highway out the Interstate; Monday Night Football; someone throwin' an impromptu barbecue; Old Grand-Dad bourbon; shapely legs, and wild flowin' hair flared out across a motel-room pillow . . .

I look up from my patch of tomatoes and see furtive movement over by the farm truck. I watch as two cons fling somethin' on to the truck. It's not a tomato crate. It's limp and life-sized. One of the guys, who I recognize as a Tennessee Stomper, climbs on to the truck bed, where the wooden sides obscure him. The other keeps a lookout for guards.

Wayne is a few rows over from me. I go over to him and tell him I'm not sure but I think the Stompers have his girl-friend.

Wayne turns to see. I figure, for sure, he's gonna go apeshit.

But he doesn't say anything, just watches, restin' his chin

on the end of a rake handle. The biker climbs off the truck bed and appears to be doin' up the buttons on his jump-suit. The other Stomper climbs on to the truck and takes his place.

Suddenly, Wayne says, 'I hope none of this is reflecting badly on you.'

That strikes me as uncharacteristic for him to say and when I look at his face he doesn't look like a scared punk anymore. He studies me, as if he's about to confide some-thin'.

'At first I was really scared about being here,' he says.

'What?'

'I never thought of myself as someone who would ever end up in prison. And I knew it would chew me up.'

'What *are* you in for?' I asked.

'Forging VINs.' Vehicle Identification Numbers. An age-old used-car salesman's scam.

'You're a car salesman?'

'Dealer,' he corrects me. 'Salesmen just take orders. I moved fifteen hundred units a year on and off the lot. Until I got busted for the VIN thing.'

By now, some of the other men have put down their tools and are movin', minnowlike, toward the truck. Wayne watches them detachedly. I realize I'm talkin' to a completely different Wayne Pennegar.

He continues: 'When I got sentenced, I had to think of some way to protect myself once I was inside. I figured if I'm in a biker gang, no one will fuck with me. I knew a couple of guys in the Satan Chasers, guys I'd sold trucks to – given 'em a good deal too. I thought maybe I had an in with 'em.'

'An "in"? With a biker gang!'

'Look. I wasn't exactly thinkin' clearly, alright? Christ, I'm about to go off to prison!'

'Yeah, I understand.'

'I go over to their clubhouse, this garage-type place, and ask to join, just like that. This big hairy dude, this walking bag of scar tissue, says, "Sure, you can be a Satan Chaser . . . but you got to go through the initiation." The next thing I know they got me pinned down and they're shoving Barbie in my ass. They're all standin' around laughin'. Afterwards, they give me a photo and they show me the door. So now, I'm waddling down the street with my ass on fire and I can still hear 'em all behind me, this evil laughter. Now I'm confused, because I'm not *exactly* sure if this means I'm a *bona fide* Satan Chaser or not. I mean, maybe the Barbie business was their idea of, you know, a little joke.'

'I'm pretty sure it was a joke, Wayne.'

'That's what's going on in my head. But my ass, *my extremely tender ass*, pipes up and says, "I don't know about you but as far as I'm concerned, *that was an initiation*." Fine, I'm a Satan Chaser. The day before I reported for sentencing, I go to a tattoo parlor and the dumb sonofabitch misspells *Satan*. I'm thinkin' this doesn't get worse.'

A dozen cons have gathered around the truck, jostling each other animatedly. The guards are at the other end of the field, talkin' among themselves, oblivious.

'When I get here, who do I run in to but two Stompers who see the tattoo and tell me they're gonna fix my little red wagon. I'd never even *heard* of the Stompers. I'm inside one day and already I've got an instant ass-kicking coming to me.' Wayne pauses and watches the commotion at the truck for a moment. There's an orderly line now, everyone waitin' for their shot at the dummy.

'After they beat me up, the bubble just burst. The time had come for me to start actin' crazy. It was the only way I was gonna make it through this.'

'So you ain't crazy at all are you?'

'Oh, I didn't say that,' he says.

Suddenly, he yells to the guards, 'Knockin' it for a loop!!'

The guards look over at him and he motions toward the truck activity. They turn and see the commotion and instantly they're movin' toward the cons, shotguns at the ready.

Now Wayne's laughin'. He turns to me and says, 'Those are some desperate sonofabitches right there.'

He throws down his rake, slaps me on the back, says 'See you on the Highway to Heaven!' and makes for the tractor. I watch him gambol across the field, his feet kickin' up clouds of dirt in the spongy loam. He reaches the tractor and doesn't look back, just clambers on, starts it up and steers for the fence. He plows right through, draggin' a steel honeycomb of twisted metal behind him. I watch him go until he's just a blue shimmer, like a flame in a pilot light, bouncin' off into the distance.

Brenda #2

I never meant to marry my second wife. I only meant to rob her. Or rather, her home, which was a trailer. I was twenty-eight and driftin' from motel to motel, all of them out on the Knoxville Highway. I spent my days watchin' *Let's Make a Deal*, and robbin' mobile homes. When I say 'robbin' mobile homes', I don't mean breakin' into them. I mean I *stole* mobile homes.

I had a gunmetal-gray Ford F-350 with heavy-duty suspension, lifters, thrush pipes and custom tow package. My buddy, Chopper McFadgeon, had a buddy who knew someone at the Bank of Knoxville who would sneak us a weekly list of foreclosures. We'd go through the list and circle the address of some deadbeat trailer owner who was about to be evicted for non-payment. We'd find the address and if the owner was out we'd just haul the thing away. The owner would come home to an empty concrete pad and figure the damn thing had been repossessed. They never thought to call the cops. That was our going racket that summer.

Some folks like to call a trailer a 'caravan', but there's a difference. A caravan has wheels, implyin' a kind of nomadic superiority. A trailer never goes nowhere. A collection of trailers is called a Trailer Park, which is laughable, unless your idea of a 'park' is ten fly-blown acres of patchy dirt, abandoned shopping carts, rusty appliances, moldering trash heaps, broken-down cars and a muffled chorus of tequila-fueled wifebeating coming from inside each metal container. That ain't a 'park'. That's a Redneck Riviera.

Calling a trailer a 'mobile home' is also stretchin' it a bit. It's not a 'home' if you can break into it with a can opener. Sometimes, in places like Florida or Southern California, you might come across a pleasant lookin' trailer community, with tidy gardens and shiny little awnings. Those ain't real trailer parks. Those are retirement communities, and the people inside them are just easin' into the idea of spendin' eternity in a small box.

While me and Chopper were sittin' there casin' a trailer, he'd envision elaborate architectural changes. It wasn't enough for Chopper to just slap some paint on 'em and resell 'em. He liked to spiff 'em up a bit, put a little pride and detail into it. 'Never do nothin' half-assed,' he liked to say.

'Whaddya reckon, Chopper?' I said one mornin'.

We were parked under a big crooked willow in some ratshit trailer park in South Knoxville, eyein' a walnut-brown FletcherCraft that had all the kerb appeal of a UPS truck. It sat on breezeblocks, with creosoted railroad ties for steps leadin' up to the front door.

'Hell, it's an empty canvas,' said Chopper. 'We could do a little Edwardian number on it. Wrought-iron ogee work around the windows. Maybe some dentil molding or cornices for dimension.'

Chopper enjoyed throwin' around words like *ogee* as if

he were Frank Lloyd Wright or some other famous fuckin' architect. He probably picked it up playin' scrabble.

'What's *Edwardian* mean anyway?' I said.

He looked at me like I was pathetic.

'*King* Edward. *In the style of King Edward.*'

'King Edward lived in a trailer?' I asked. I couldn't resist windin' Chopper up, particularly since he once told me he'd earned a 'Filigree' in Architecture from East Tennessee State University.

'Fuck you and anybody who looks like you,' he said and, by way of punctuation, shot a reedy brown bolus of tobacco juice out the truck window.

Just then the door to the trailer opened and a gal stepped out. She stood there on the steps for a moment, like maybe she was just takin' in the mornin' before headin' off to work. What really knocked me out was the getup she was wearin': a buckskin loincloth, waistcoat and moccasin boots that went halfway up her calves. I'd say she was about 5'2. I'd say she came in at around 140 pounds. And I'd say she was stacked with a set of shame cushions that, given the slightest breeze, probably would have undulated like one of them executive desk toys. Billiard tits. By that, I mean you wanted to take her to a pool hall just to watch 'em bobble every time she made a shot.

I knew she wasn't married because she didn't have a black eye. But I knew I was *gonna* marry her.

You know, of course, when you see an attractive gal, a miniature devil and angel appear on your shoulders, like in cartoons. And the devil, reckless romantic that he is, will lean into your ear and whisper, '*Oh man, you got to jump on this like white on rice!*' And the angel, the voice of reason – who keeps a runnin' file of all the times you did this before and ended up in Rockbottom, population: one – leans into

51

your other ear and says, *'Take time to know her.'* And the angel is right. You *know* the angel is right.

Well, I don't get those particular individuals on my shoulders. What I get is a miniature Johnny Cash, about an inch high, dressed in black. And when she stepped out of the trailer that fine Tennessee mornin', I distinctly heard the miniature Johnny Cash in my ear say *'If you don't try to fuck her, son, I will!'*

Then, I realized, I'd already tried. Ten, maybe twelve, years ago, back when I was marginally a student and high school was just a bad party where you had to bring your own refreshments. I remembered her name was Brenda somethingorother – a goofy last name that had earned her undeserved ridicule. She was just a garden-variety peroxide blonde, with that slack, slightly canine posture you see in lots of poor Southern girls. Later, when I got within groping distance, I'd detected, beneath her Maybelline veneer, the skin texture of a basketball.

But man, had she blossomed. Standin' on the steps now, in the sunlight, she looked incendiary.

Chopper saw it come over me, I guess, because he didn't say anything. We both watched her kind of lightly descend from the steps, round the corner of the trailer and disappear toward the main highway. I could've lingered there all mornin' watchin' her fantastic legs walk away. Never forget your first view of a woman walkin' away. You'll likely see it again.

Chopper eased his corpulent hulk out of the truck and walked purposefully up to the trailer door. He knocked and waited for a human or dog response. Then we matter-of-factly went to work. I couldn't stop thinkin' about the buckskin gal.

How to steal a trailer: Remove the skirting around the trailer's underside. Disconnect the propane tanks, electrical wirin', and water lines. Crawl up under the trailer and unbolt the toilet stack from the sewer pipe. Now the thing is off all its life support.

The most important tool a trailer thief needs – and as far as I know, we were the *only* trailer thieves – is a mobile-home axle which, unless you're a professional transporter, you'll need to build yourself. It takes two men to carry it. Anyway, once you've got your axle positioned underneath, bolt it to the tie-beam, jack up the trailer, slip on the tires and hook the whole thing up to your truck hitch. Drive away like you own it. Normally a team of professional movers spend half a day preppin' a mobile home for transport. We could do it in thirty minutes.

We did our work crisply with no concern for pryin' eyes. People in trailer parks see homes get repossessed all the time. It ain't all that unusual.

While Chopper was preparin' the hitch, I went up the steps of the trailer and jimmied my way inside.

Buttkracken. Her name was Brenda *Buttkracken.* This I got from her check stubs. She worked at the Rib Raft, which was just up the highway a bus stop or two. She made a hundred eight dollars a week, after taxes. Plus tips, I imagined.

Not surprisingly, the trailer was practically empty. I can't count the number of times me and Chopper would steal a gleamin' new trailer, stickers still on the windows, and later, when we had a look inside, see that the owners didn't have a goddamn pot to piss in. Lawn chairs for furniture, Kraft dinners in the cupboard. Frisbees for plates, shoehorns for spoons. Spent all the money on the box and there was nothing left to put inside it. The nicer the frame, the emptier the interior. Not unlike a good-lookin' woman.

Far as I could tell, Brenda wasn't a methamphetamine chef or an alcoholic slob. From the creditors' letters I found she was just a gal strugglin' to make it by. But she did own

53

a cheap Realistic stereo and, on a mirror, fixed in place by cellophane tape, was a Narvel Crump album, which I found disturbing.

Narvel Crump was the current toast of Country Music. Not *real* Country Music, like Merle Haggard or Johnny Cash, but the kind of saccharine hypoglycemic, diabetes-inducin' twaddle that Nashville tries to *pass off* as Country Music. Narvel was one of those swarthy, wax-shouldered Hat Acts whose syrupy crooning drove a certain kind of female fan moist. His current hit was a song called 'Don't Crush an Angel' which featured the lyrics:

> I gently place a pillow
> Beneath her head where it can't slip
> I don't want to crush her halo
> Every time I kiss her lips.

That Narvel Crump album should have warned me off Brenda right there. But, like I said, I was a little bit smitten.

I went outside and told Chopper we weren't gonna steal the trailer.

He looked baffled.

'What the hell you talkin' about we ain't gonna steal it?' he said. 'It's ready to go!'

'Leave it. We'll find us another.'

'Jus' 'cause she's a piece of ass? That ain't professional!'

'Unhook the trailer, Chopper.'

Chopper wouldn't hear it. He went to my truck, climbed into the driver's seat and started the motor.

'Get outta my truck!' I warned him. All around us, dogs, sensing our unprofessionalism, had begun barkin' loudly. I looked over and saw a lady across the way come out on her porch.

'You comin' or ain't ya?' Chopper called out, gunning the engine. This wasn't the place for a Mexican standoff. I went around and climbed in the passenger side.

The trailer groaned behind us, the truck suspension strugglin' with the excess weight. I always got a titanic rush feelin' a mobile home come off its moorings. I would think to myself, 'There's petty crime and then there's crime that's actually visible from outer space'. And this was crime visible from outer space.

When we got to the junction with the highway, Chopper stopped the truck, climbed out and went around back to hang a Wide Load banner. Then he came around to my side, flung open the door and dragged me out of the truck. Quite deftly, for a man shaped like a sea cow, he managed to collapse his entire weight against me, pinning me to the side of the truck.

'You stupid sonofabitch,' he snarled. 'If you ever pull that kind of shit again, I'll smack you so fuckin' hard you'll starve to death turning cartwheels, un'erstand? I'll pull your fuckin' eyeballs out on stalks. I will make it possible for you to be an eyewitness to your own beatin'.'

Every word he sputtered, almost *visibly* brown from the stench of chewing tobacco, burned my face. Then with extreme vitality, he hurled me on to the pavement. I landed on my face and, for a moment, forgot where I was. By the time I looked up I could see my own checkbone swelling into vision, and, beyond that, Chopper chugging back around to the driver's side.

'Coulda gone all day without this shit,' he muttered, then climbed inside and threw the gears. Sprawled on the ground, I watched him drive off in my truck.

*   *   *

55

It was about a mile-and-a-half walk to the Rib Raft. Brenda was workin' the Salad Canoe, ferryin' tubs of coleslaw and potato salad in and out of the kitchen. They'd made her wear a ridiculous coonskin cap.

I sat down at a table near the kitchen, next to three hefty businessman types who had their sleeves rolled up and were tearin' into a side of ribs like drunken midwives. They seemed to be engaged in some kind of lusty workplace discussion.

'Guess who's suin' for sexual harassment?' the largest one said. 'Jugs, over in accountin'.' Then Brenda whirled past the table and he called out, 'Hey Pocahontas, how 'bout rustlin' us up s'more paper napkins.'

I didn't like his proprietary attitude. I leaned over and very measuredly said, 'Her name ain't Pocahontas.'

They all stopped chewin' and eyed me uneasily.

'Christ, buddy, what tore into your face?' the fattest businessman muttered.

Brenda stopped beside me.

'How ya doin', Sizzlechest?' I said, puttin' my best foot forward.

She didn't recognize me. Or else pretended not to.

'What can I get you, besides some gauze.'

'Brenda Buttkracken,' I said.

'I know you?'

'Yeah. Otis Lee Crenshaw.'

'Nothin's comin' to mind.'

'We went out a few times. Back in school.'

'You played football?'

'No.'

'Track and field?'

'No?'

'Photography club?'

'No?'

56

'Did we fuck?'

'Not for my lack of tryin'.'

'Thank God. Well, what can I get ya, Otis Lee Crenshaw?'

'I've stolen your trailer.'

She sat down on the edge of the table. To this day, I can still remember what she smelled like: cinnamon and butter. As a rule, the overpowering industrial waft of the Rib Raft's world-famous barbecue sauce generally made its patrons' eyes run like open sores. Brenda's fragrance seemed to cut right through that.

'You wanna run that by me again?'

'Your trailer. Brown one, right?'

'Yeah?'

'Well, I've stolen it. As a favor.'

She waited a long time to say anything. Finally, 'Alright, I think it's comin' back to me. You were the class punchbag.'

The napkinless businessmen were tryin' to listen in to our exchange. ''Scuse us, but we're in kind of a bind over here,' one of them called out, wavin' his greasy fingers helplessly.

'If you fellas had bothered to notice,' I informed them, 'it's a Life-on-the-Mississippi theme goin' on in here.'

'Yeah?'

'So why don't you go jump in the fuckin' river.'

That quieted them down.

'I got an inside source,' I said to Brenda, 'that you're gonna get repossessed next week. So my buddy and me stole your home. When we're done with it, no one will even recognize it. You can move it anywhere you like. Free and clear.'

She let that settle in. 'Why would you do such a thing?'

'I don't know. I saw you this mornin'. Standin' outside your trailer. I thought you was the sexiest thing I ever laid eyes on.'

'You in the habit of stealin' girls' homes and givin' them back? Some kind of extravagant come on?'

'Nah. I wouldn't say that.'

'You wouldn't say that. Me, I got a bit of a wild streak. But you're plain crazy.'

She stood up, smoothin' her uniform. Man, what cleavage. If I'd been Lassie, I wouldn't've come out of that cave until every last kid was rescued.

'Listen, I get off at seven. Come back then.'

'Alright, I will.'

'You want a frozen pork chop? That cheek don't look too good.'

'Nah thanks,' I said, standin' up. 'I'll see ya at seven.'

On my way out she called out across the restaurant.

'Hey!'

I turned.

'You ain't a musician are you?'

'Not mucha' one.'

'Encouraging,' she said.

Trailer thieves, but not musicians, I thought. Some judge of character she was. I headed back up the highway, thinkin' to myself that a good romance can always use some tension to kickstart it.

'I no longer see you as the kind of executive material I'm accustomed to workin' with,' Chopper said, when I came for my truck. 'Take your truck and evacuate the premises.'

I'd had to hitchhike out to his warehouse, an old Cessna hangar he'd stolen, section by section, from the Sevier County Executive Airport. Brenda's trailer now took up most of the inside. He'd stripped the exterior. Now it was a shell, the color of a dirty spoon. The inside was gutted.

Sheet paneling, carpet, ceiling tiles, all gone, cleaned out like a jack-o'-lantern.

He was standin' by a workbench, cleanin' the nozzle on a paint sprayer. I was keepin' some distance between us, holdin' a claw hammer from his toolbox. Just for insurance.

'*Vacate*,' I said.

'Say hun'h?'

'*Vacate* the premises. You said "*evacuate*".' Nothin' annoyed me more than people who thought they had a bigger vocabulary than me.

'Yeah. Well, you got my drift, anyway. And who said you could touch my tools?'

'About the trailer.'

'What about it?'

'The girl. I told her we stole it, Chopper.'

He brought the spray nozzle up to his mouth and blew into it to make sure it was clear of paint. Then, he casually hurled the entire canister at me. It missed and exploded against a wall, leaving a vicious green splotch. I guessed Seafoam or maybe Pale Avocado – not a flattering color for the trailer given Brenda's complexion.

'You little shitbiscuit,' he seethed.

I stood my ground.

'Listen up, Chopper. We do it up real nice. Paint, trim, interior, the whole shebang. And new ID plates. Then, we give it back to her.'

'*Give* it back to her?' He looked wild eyed.

'That's what I said. Next trailer we steal, you can keep all the money.'

'Well, ain't that mighty noble of you. Unfortunately, I've already sold your little love shack.'

'To who?'

'Some wholesaler over in Oak Ridge. Wants to give it to

his daughter-in-law as a weddin' gift.' Maybe he was lyin', maybe not.

'Well, we'll hafta steal it back again.'

Chopper's face went plum red with fury.

'The fuck we're gonna steal it again!' he bellowed, and came at me, misting tobacco juice. 'There's a saturation point to my tolerance and you've just crossed it!'

I had a solid grip on the claw hammer. Before he could reach me, I said, 'If we don't give it back, she's gonna call the cops.'

He seemed to wither in front of me. Truthfully, I didn't think for one second Brenda would have called the cops. I think she appreciated what I was tryin' to do for her. But it was sure the right thing to say to keep Chopper from drenchin' me with tobacco-juice spray again.

'Well, you've managed to fuck things for both of us now, haven't you?'

'That girl,' I said, 'is my future wife.'

He shook his head.

'Well, all I got to say's you better bang her like Hoss Cartwright on the Pussy Ponderosa. 'Cause if you don't keep her happy, we're all goin' down the river.'

I grabbed some of Brenda's clothes and her Maybelline products and stuffed them into an overnight bag so she'd have something to change into. Then I stopped off at the liquor store for a twelve-pack of bottled Bud. I killed three of them on the way to the Rib Raft.

'Well aren't you the sweetest thing comin' up the pike,' she said, when I picked her up. Hard to tell if that was sarcastic or not. Then she sprang into the back seat to divest herself of the rawhide getup.

'I can't wait to get out of this stupid uniform,' she chirped.

'Say, you reckon you got enough empties back here?' The back-seat floor was full of beer bottles.

'Those are floor chimes,' I said, tryin' to get a peek at her in the rear view. She re-emerged in denim jeans and a low-cut T-shirt. She squeezed my hand and seemed to resonate an expansive good cheer you wouldn't expect from someone whose home had just been pilfered.

We drove over to where her trailer used to be. She stared at the empty concrete pad and let out a low, mordant whistle.

'I'll be damned,' she said, impressed. 'You've got some balls.' She leaned back against the truck door. 'Just where am I supposed to stay now?'

'Well at the risk of soundin' abrupt, I got a motel room out the highway a bit.'

I didn't bother to tell her the motel was called the Tender Trap – someone's idea of a truckers' honeymoon palace that had never quite taken off. Red velvet furniture, heart-shaped tubs, pictures of matadors on the wall. It looked like a whorehouse that had lost its fundin'.

'Move in just like that?'

'That's the idea.'

'Have you been through my stuff?'

'There wasn't much.'

'I'm goin' through somewhat spartan circumstances right now.'

'You ain't gotta apologize.'

I could feel her eyes borin' into me, tryin' to figure me out. 'So what's your story, mister?' she said, and before I got around to it, hers spilled out.

She'd gone down to Florida after high school. Lived there for ten years. Then her momma died, so she'd come back to East Tennessee, where the cost of livin' was cheap and she could dive comfortably into the white-trash labor pool. She'd put a down payment on a trailer, got a waitressin' job at the Rib Raft, and, for the first time, felt like she was on her own.

'Then, along comes Narvel Crump,' she said, 'the last of my hard bargains.'

'Narvel Crump?'

'Yeah, him. A real piece of dogshit.'

'You own his album.'

'To remind me of what a reptile he is.' She said this with the resignation of someone with an incurable affliction. 'He's a big star now and he *still* has everything I own. If I could find him, I'd serve him a mercury omelet. I'll bet that's more about me than you wanna know.'

All I could think to ask was if Narvel's line about putting 'a pillow beneath her head' was written with her in mind.

She bristled. 'How the fuck should I know? I ain't seen any *inspiration* checks in the mail.' She took a long swig of Bud and gazed pensively at the empty trailer pad.

'At least he didn't put your name in a song,' I said.

'What's that mean?'

'"Brenda Buttkracken". That's not exactly "Eleanor Rigby".'

'Who?'

'You know, "Eleanor Rigby".'

'I don't know too many people around here anymore.'

'Or "Billy Joe MacAllister".'

She stared at me.

'In *Ode to Billy Joe*. The poor girl's forced to throw her baby off a bridge. There's no need to name names.'

She just kept starin'.

'My gut instinct,' she said, 'is that I'm ever gonna understand maybe half of what you're talkin' about.'

I tried to get back on track.

'So how did you get mixed up with Narvel Crump anyway?'

'I met him one night at the Blue Parrot. He wasn't no star then, just a honky-tonk shitkicker playin' for buckets of loose change. I reckon he was kinda cute. And I was sufficiently convinced he didn't have enough talent to be any kind of threat to my independence.'

'What do you mean?'

'What I mean is, I never wanted no one to look after me.'

She lit up a cigarette. I lit up a cigarette.

'Anyway, he saw my trailer and I reckon he thought to himself "carrion", and moved right in. Never paid a dime in rent. Ran up my long-distance bill tryin' to phone his way into show business. One day he shows up with this waterbed and some fake horsehide livin' room furniture, which it turns out he'd hijacked off a delivery truck. And the whole time I'm thinkin', "What am I doin'?". He's a fucking barnacle. He didn't even bother to unpack the furniture. Just razored off the cartons and the couch sat there in this little island of cardboard. That's what a useless sonofabitch he was.'

She fired her cigarette end emphatically out the window and waved at the smoke dismissively. The whole time she was tellin' me this, I was sneakin' glances at her wondrous cleavage. I mean, I was *listenin'*, but I was also just amazed by how a void could be created from so much volume. And how a man could be attracted to what was, essentially, sheer nothingness.

'You listenin' or preoccupied?'

'I'm listenin'.'

'One afternoon I come home and the trailer is surrounded by a sea of mud. I mean, it ain't rained for weeks right? And the trailer is listin' to one side like it's gonna sink. I go inside. The place is empty. The furniture's gone. The waterbed is gone. He's drained it – a hundred gallons – right out the bedroom window. And there's a note sayin' he's gone to

Nashville to make a demo. And I'm standin' in this empty trailer, sinkin' into the earth and thinkin' to myself, no man is ever gonna live up to what I expect of them but they always manage to get me to lower myself to what they expect.'

When a woman tells you a hard-luck story like that, you would do best to just listen and try to offer a little comfort. What you shouldn't do is offer advice. Because that puts you in the position of havin' to act on it. Which is stupidly what I did.

'I'll find him,' I said.

'Narvel?'

'Yeah. It can't be that hard.'

She crossed her arms and studied me. 'And then what?'

'Get your waterbed back,' I said.

'We'll see about that,' she said. 'It would help if I had somewhere to put it, wouldn't it? When do I get my trailer back?'

'Soon's my buddy's done fixin' it up.' 'Buddy, my ass,' I thought. There was no point in mentionin' that complications with Chopper had set in.

'That would be about the nicest thing anyone's done for me lately,' she said, dryly.

We downed at least three Buds apiece and sat there listenin' to the sounds of the trailer park night comin' to life. It was the purification hour. Doors thundered on their hinges, dogs yelped, car engines screamed, husbands and wives verbally peeled flesh off of each other. Every metal container was an echo chamber. TVs were cranked up so loud they sounded angry. Stereos dueled. Roger Miller and Lynyrd Skynyrd battled it out for supremacy. Sometimes two people remember their first song together. Ours was a hybrid: 'No phone, no food, no pets . . . Gimme three steps,

64

gimme three steps, mister, and you won't see me no more
. . . I ain't got no cigarettes . . .'

'Nice rig,' Brenda said, splayin' her lacquered nails across
the dash.

'It's a bench seat,' I said.

'Yeah? So?'

'So. You ain't gotta sit all the way over there.'

She slid over and I tried to kiss her. Unfortunately, my
softball-sized cheek kept her lips somewhat at bay. Instead,
she crawled under my arm, and at last I was able to get my
hands on to God's little half acres. For maybe five seconds.
Then, abruptly, she disengaged herself and twisted off
another Bud cap.

'That fuckin' Narvel didn't even *have* a truck,' she said.
'Drove a camper van. Where's that in his songs?'

I was too drunk to drive, which is when I do my best
drivin'. When we got to my motel, she took a look around,
threw up in the heart-shaped tub, and then put some rent
money on the top of the TV.

'You don't hafta pay rent,' I said.

'Yes I do,' she replied. 'Look, this is purely temporary,
you know.'

'No it ain't,' I said.

The thing about Love at First Sight is, you know your heart
has written a check your brain can't cash but you try to
take it to the bank anyway. The way Brenda smiled at me,
those tits, that cinnamon buttery smell, the fact that she
needed somethin' from me – hell, all women need somethin' from you, don't they? Else they wouldn't get involved
at all. But it's better if the thing they need from you is
specific. It's better if what they need from you is *somethin'
back*.

Up until I met Brenda, I would've told you Love at First Sight is just a lot of rhapsodic drivel – the kind of thing schmaltzmeisters like Narvel Crump plunder for a livin'.

Now I was seein' it as a nifty device for circumventing the usual shit you have to go through to *arrive* at Love: flirting, plotting, makin' points, playin' hard-to-get, scupperin' every last ounce of dignity in your soul. Well, fuck that for a laugh! If Love is a waste of time, at least Love at First Sight is an *express* waste of time.

'You kind of remind me of my old man,' she'd said, back there at the trailer park. Man, that threw me.

'I mean, I only ever remember him from Polaroids. But you look like him.'

'Yeah? Good lookin' fella was he?'

'I don't know. He was good around the eyes. He was a sonofabitch, but you wouldn't know that from a picture, would you?'

I don't suppose it's occurred to people who've fallen in Love that maybe they were *poised* for it. Lookin' back, it's possible there was a confluence in my life that meant I was ready to fall for the next person who passed by. To be honest, I was pretty fuckin' lonely. Lonely enough to lick ashtrays because it was kind of like kissin' a smoker. Horny enough to dry hump a cactus. And tired of livin' in cheap motels, with their ice machine death rattles, truck headlights searin' through the curtains in the middle of the night. Swollen ashtrays and scattered bottles. The sordid knowledge that a million strangers have left their transient stain on the bedspread, the carpets, the furniture. Shit, everyone needs a home.

In the septic undertow of my childhood memories, the person who stands out the most is my grandaddy. He died when I was fairly young, but I remember the thrill of him takin' me to the Pioneers' meetings.

The Pioneers were some kind of civic fraternity of rancorous oldtimers who, under the guise of raisin' money for crippled kids, gathered weekly at the Knoxville Civic Lodge to drink and play Texas Hold 'em. My grandaddy used to take me along and let me run wild.

And twice a year, Easter and Labor Day, I got to march in the Pioneers' parade. We got all dressed up in our buckskin finery and coonskin caps and rode down Main Street on a log float, shootin' muskets full of miniature Tootsie Rolls at the passin' throngs. At the end of the day, whatever Tootsie Rolls were left over, I got to take home.

This is more attention than my folks ever paid to me. Hell, they never even knew where I was most of the time and when I got home, all excited about my swag, my momma would just grunt summarily and go back to watching *Perry Mason*.

My Old Man was never around to witness any of this. He was off bein' a lab rat.

So what's this got to do with Love at First Sight? Well, you don't hafta be Sigfried and Freud to figure it out, do you? There's Brenda in her rawhide outfit, standin' in front of a trailer. Not much different than the kind of trailers I grew up in. She's young and pretty but, more profoundly, somethin' in her harkens back to my grandaddy.

They say sometimes guys like to marry women that remind them of their mommas. True, maybe, but what if it's more complex than that? What if Momma spent all her time *covering* for Daddy, because Daddy was always out drinkin' all night? Well then, now you're not lookin' to marry Momma anymore; you're lookin' to marry Daddy, aren't you?

And suppose you meet a gal who is lookin' for her daddy,

because *he* wasn't around when *she* was growin' up? And she sees it in you. So now you're daddy to a gal who's your daddy. Which makes you your own grandfather.

Brenda made me feel like the person I always wanted to be. My grandaddy. And I think that's why I fell in love with her.

Monday the followin' week, I called Chopper.

'What's goin' on with the trailer?' I said.

'It's gone. The wholesaler came down here this mornin' with a rig. Paid up and carted it away.'

'Any problems?'

'Well, there was a little resistance, but he came around.'

'What kind of resistance?'

'It weren't nothin'. Little dustup over some of the design changes I made. Anyway, your half o' the money's sittin' here in a mitre box.'

'I don't want the money, Chopper. We got to get that trailer back.'

I could hear him sigh and spit on the other end.

'This ain't fuckin' professional,' he said, and hung up.

Maybe a week later, I was walkin' Brenda down Polk Street, content as all get out. Suddenly she wheeled around, diggin' at my arm.

'That guy just ran his hand up my skirt,' she said.

'Who? Point him out.'

She indicated. The man was in a velour jogging suit. I saw the back of his thick head bobbin' above the crowd. She turned back and fixed her gaze on me, expectantly.

I've never been one for throwin' the first punch. But I thought to myself, 'This won't do,' and went back and decked the guy, who sprawled across the sidewalk. I looked over and saw my reflection, etched like a cinematic after-image, in a bookshop window. Somehow, it just didn't look like me. The man sat up and rubbed his jaw, trying to put two and two together. A small, percolating crowd had gathered now.

'Popped the dude, good!' I heard someone say.

Brenda stood there at a distance watchin' the whole thing. I caught up with her and she wouldn't look me in the eye.

'That was just exemplary white-trash behavior,' she said, but I could see the corners of her mouth turned up slightly. We kept walkin' and I couldn't think of a damned thing else to say, so finally I just asked her to marry me.

'That's ridiculous.'

'No it ain't. You won't do better than me.'

'Normally there's a ring that accompanies this type of gesture.'

'A *ring*? I'm givin' you your trailer back.'

'Give me my trailer back first. Then I'll think about it.'

'Marry me first. Then I'll give you your trailer back.'

'Give me the trailer back or I'll call the cops.'

'*Call* the cops. I'll call the finance company – tell 'em where they can find your trailer.'

'While you're being assraped in your cell on a regular basis.'

'At least I'll have a bed.'

Then, after a moment she said, 'Oh hell, alright.'

We drove to the Sevier County Justice of the Peace, filled out the forms and, just like that, I became my own grandad.

Several days later, Brenda #2 admitted that the guy on Polk Street hadn't done anything. The business with the hand up her skirt, she'd just made that up to test my resolve. I thought marriage was supposed to be about tyin' a knot. But I had this distinct feeling of somethin' startin' to unravel.

*   *   *

69

The *News Sentinel* ran a tiny story on the back page:

> Residents of trailer parks in South Knoxville have
> been warned that mobile-home thieves may be
> operating in their area. City Police Chief Cecil
> VanWerter believes the scheme involves trailers
> that have been slated for foreclosure. The thefts
> were uncovered after a semi-resident of the
> Oakmount Trailer Court told police he awoke to
> discover his mobile home 'moving'.
>
> Darryl Toll, 36, said, 'I was taking a nap on my
> brother-in-law's couch. When I woke up we was
> sitting in the middle of an intersection. I managed
> to get out the front door before the light changed.'
> Toll said the trailer was pulled by two men in a
> gray heavy-duty pickup truck.
>
> 'I couldn't get the plate number on account of
> my glasses was in my shirt pocket that was still
> in the trailer,' Toll said.
>
> 'The trailers are probably being sold to buyers
> who have no idea they're stolen,' said Chief
> VanWerter.

I drove over to Chopper's place to tell him we needed to
lay low, but he'd already seen the article.

'Leave the truck with me for a few days,' he said, and
drove me home. Now I was stuck at the Tender Trap with
no wheels. I watched *Let's Make a Deal* about ten times a
day and waited for Brenda to finish work and then we'd
have to *walk* to a fuckin' roadhouse for a beer. She wouldn't
shut up about the goddamned trailer. I hadn't told her
Chopper had sold it. I was tryin' to buy time. The day she
bought it, she'd had a picture taken of herself standin' in
front of it. Now the picture was taped to the motel mirror

70

where I couldn't avoid seein' it. It reminded me of that day I'd first seen her step outside. But it was unsettling, like a valentine card from a loanshark. Her few belongings sat in a tenuous pile in the corner of the room. She wouldn't even use a closet. Late at night, driftin' off, I thought I heard her slipping icy innuendoes in my ear. 'Fish or cut bait,' for example.

Three days later, Chopper showed up at the motel. 'I got somethin' to show you,' he announced.

We drove out to the warehouse in his Oldsmobile. He threw open the doors and there was my truck.

Only now it was a lurid metallic blue. And, as if that wasn't gaudy enough, he'd airbrushed a pair of ducks on the doors. The ducks were fucking in mid-flight. Underneath were the words 'Fly United', in the distinctive logo of United Airlines. He'd seen it on a novelty T-shirt and must've thought it was the most magnificent joke he'd ever encountered.

'Duckfuck truck!' he cackled. 'Whaddya reckon?'

I threw a claw hammer straight at his head, just missin'. He dropped to the floor and scurried behind the tailgate for cover.

'C'mon!' he yelled. 'I spent three days on it!' I detected in his voice a genuine pain of spurned artistry.

'Put it back the way it was,' I said.

'That is a pristine metalflake job, you ungrateful son-ofabitch!' he screamed, then scrambled, crab-like, across the floor, grabbed the claw hammer, and fired it straight back at my head. It whistled past and clanged off the wall. Now it was my turn again. I picked it up and this time came straight at him. He scuttled backward until he was trapped against the wall. I could have put it right into his skull.

'What cop in his right mind would suspect this truck now?' he said, desperate to reason. 'It's *show* quality.'

Then, with skillful precision, he fired a stream of tobacco juice through his teeth and right on to my foot.

'I never do nothing half-assed,' he said.

I forced Chopper into the truck and we drove twenty-five miles to Oak Ridge to find Brenda's trailer. Everyone we passed pointed at the ducks on the door.

On the way, Chopper told me a story he'd heard about a moose up in Vermont who'd become infatuated with a cow.

'Fell head over heels for the thing. Followed it around all day. The moose would bed down in the pasture at night right beside this damn cow. Wouldn't even let the farmer who owned the thing near it.'

'Ain't that somethin',' I said.

'Seventy-six days. The moose followed that cow around for seventy-six days.'

'Then what?'

'They had to shoot it. Just like I'm gonna do to you.'

We cruised through at least six trailer parks in Oak Ridge, lookin' for the trailer. It was turnin' dusk and I was worried that if we got there, the newlyweds – the wholesaler's son and daughter-in-law – would be there. I wondered if stealin' a trailer with people inside constituted kidnapping. That's all I needed, another involuntary kidnapping rap.

Suddenly Chopper called out, 'There it is!'

'Where?'

Then I saw it.

It would be almost impossible to describe the psychopathic extravagance of what Chopper had done to Brenda's trailer. For starters, the front entrance was now encased in a rotunda. As for the rest of the trailer, he had mounted Doric columns at approximately two-foot intervals all around the outside, and the roof was flanked on either end by a pair of six-foot-high buzzards – plaster, I suspected. Chopper's budget probably would have stopped short of marble. Nonetheless, the buzzards appeared to be tryin' to lift the whole bizarre contraption off the ground and carry it aloft.

Occasionally, within all the ornate trappings, the original trailer still managed to lurk through. It reminded me, vaguely, of the building on the back of a nickel.

If you're wondrin' how I'm familiar with terms like 'rotunda' and 'Doric', it's because Chopper dragged me from the truck, in a depraved, crippling headlock, and personally gave me a close-up tour of his handiwork.

'See that? That's a fuckin' Palladian window, assface!' he said, and made a motion as if to push my head through it, then changed his mind.

'I spent *two days* on that!'

Next, he muscled me over to the entrance and squashed my face up against the freshly painted portico.

'Now, I want you to closely inspect the craftsmanship of this rotunda. It's neo-fucking-classic . . .'

From my vantage point, it was certainly easy enough to determine the thing was made from wood, not plaster. I gasped for air and gargled saliva and wondered how I was ever goin' to explain this monstrosity to Brenda.

Later, as I was lyin' on the ground, tryin' to feel my trachea expand back to its normal shape, Chopper pushed a fresh thatch of tobacco behind his teeth and stated, emphatically, that we *weren't* going to steal the trailer.

'It's too heavy for your puny truck,' he said. 'Besides, I *just know* them newlyweds inside is thrilled to death with my handiwork.'

After we got back to Knoxville, Chopper gave me the money I had comin' to me. I never saw him again until the arraignment.

*　　*　　*

Headin' to the Tender Trap, I wondered what I was gonna tell Brenda. I didn't have enough money to buy her a new trailer. A down payment, maybe, but then I wasn't exactly what you would call a good credit risk. In short, I was sensationally and irreversibly fucked.

I've said this before. Love at First Sight is a bad magic trick you want to believe is real. You remember that feelin' and then you bankrupt your soul tryin' to recapture it. The way you find yourself actin' all of a sudden desperate, irrational, stupid and half-assed – it ain't right.

The craziest thing was, I *hated* trailers. Spent my whole miserable childhood inside those things, and now here they were makin' my life a nightmare all over again. It's always struck me funny how all them Hollywood actors bitch and moan about the size of their trailers. But the people who *live* in 'em can't wait to get out.

I turned on the radio and wouldn't you know it, it was 'Don't Crush an Angel'. I should've turned it off but the song was so glutinous it probably would've seeped from the speakers anyway. When it ended, the DJ mentioned where Narvel was performin' next and I knew then what I had to do. I turned the truck around and headed away from town.

Fan Fair, it's called. Since anyone can remember, it's been the biggest summer attraction in Nashville.

> . . . the opportunity for Country Music's biggest performers to show their appreciation for their fans by putting on a week-long series of concerts: interacting and bonding with the people who have helped them get where they are today.

74

Or so says the playbills. Which is a load of horseshit. What it really is is a forlorn herd of rubes shellin' out $150 for the opportunity to stand in the blistering sun all day waitin' for their favorite Hick in a Hat to stroll out of an air-conditioned dressin' trailer, and run through a few perfunctory songs.

My plan – and it was pretty fuzzy at the moment – was to find Narvel. All the performers were obligated to meet their fans after their show, so I figured I'd wait in line, then shake him down for a sizeable settlement. Barring that, I would just steal his goddamned dressin' trailer.

But I never made it to Nashville. A highway patrolman pulled me over outside Lebanon.

'Know why I stopped you?' he said, hoverin' at the truck window.

'I don't know. You were lonely?'

It all went downhill from there. The reason he'd pulled me over, believe it or not, was he'd suspected some kind of copyright infringement of the ducks on the door. Not infringement of United Airlines, infringement of *the T-shirt manufacturer who'd copied the United Airlines logo*. He ran a make and model on the plates and they didn't match up to the truck color and, when he clocked the trailer axle in the back, everything began to unravel.

The last time I saw Brenda #2 was from behind a piece of perspex at Brushy Mountain State Correctional Facility. She said the whole marriage thing was probably a big mistake, but at least she'd gotten rid of that stupid last name of hers.

'I wished we'd had a chance to make it work,' she said, breakin' my fuckin' heart.

Then she stood up to leave and I watched those great getaway sticks of hers one last time.

Unspeakable Thoughts

This is what I know now: Love at First Sight is a lot of rhapsodic drivel.

It don't really happen. It's a myopic reinvention of your first meetin' with someone you eventually fell for. Maybe you first saw her through the bottom of a whiskey glass – what I like to call bourbonoculars. Maybe through a pharmaceutical haze. Perhaps, as in the case of Brenda #2, you were adrenalized from committin' a felony. All I'm sayin' is that there was somethin' in your bloodstream that magnified your perception.

Love is way too complicated to just materialize on sight. Hell, you're belittlin' the whole process by even suggestin' such a thing. Love is hard work.

No one 'falls' in Love. They jump, with suicidal abandon. All the clichés about Love seem to suggest it leads to a kind of involuntary clumsiness – beginnin' with the phrase, 'fall in love'. You ever seen someone trip over their own feet? The first thing they do is look back, usually at an imaginary object, to convince onlookers it wasn't their own oafishness that made them stumble. Why? Because no one wants to look like an idiot. Yet these same people will willingly admit

Love – a notion with no claim to weight, shape or density – caused them to lose their footing. *Love*, they claim, 'swept them off their feet'. *Love* had them 'head over heels'. *Love* turned them into a bumblin', uncoordinated clodhopper. Where's the dignity in that?

The stupidest thing you can say to someone is, 'I've fallen in Love with you'. Who wants to hear you admit you can't even stand up, that you're some kind of gimpy boneless chicken with no motor skills whatsoever?

No one's ever written an honest love song, one that says, essentially: 'I'm about to do something really stupid. I'm goin' to jump in Love.' Most love songs are whinin', mewly 'oh, I'm such a victim' copouts. Even ol' Hank Williams, a man's man if ever there was one, occasionally lapsed into Cloud Cuckold Land:

> Today I passed you on the street
> And my heart fell at your feet
> I can't help it if I'm still in love with you
> Somebody else stood by your side
> And he looked so satisfied
> I can't help it if I'm still in love with you

It's the *helpless* aspect of these songs that make them the musical equivalents of spina bifida.

I don't reckon I ever quite got over Brenda #2, but I ain't no victim. I took my lumps. It didn't work out, I moved on. If you buy into the idea that Love and Heartbreak are beyond your control, you'll always be your own gimp.

If you ask me, this whole helplessness notion started with Cupid, the original fall guy for arranged interludes. And a little prick.

If my mythology is correct, Cupid was the son of Venus

and was sent down to earth to seduce a good-lookin' gal named Psyche, who Venus was extremely jealous of. Cupid showed up at Psyche's bedside with some aphrodisiac-tipped arrows (read date rape drug). He shot her with one, then accidentally shot himself as well, the idiot. Psyche ended up in some pharmacological haze and claimed later she'd been transported to a mountain temple and promised a lot of swag. By now she had the hots for Cupid and was stalkin' him, basically. At one point, she fell out of a window, just like Chet Baker. She recovered from that and kept chasin' after Cupid until it all went screwy and she ended up dead in the middle of the road. As for Cupid, they never did convict him. He played his 'get out of jail 'cause I'm immortal' card. So there you go: he wasn't the blithe little cherub that valentine's cards have made him out to be. He was a psychopath.

When someone waxes limpidly about how 'our eyes just met and we fell for each other', you're listenin' to a liar and a fool. The eyes never give nothin' away.

If you look into someone's eyes, you're gonna see a million mixed signals – and you're gonna get it wrong. Barbara Cartland and her coterie of Spinster Porn merchants are always writin' about 'lingering gazes' and 'smoldering glances' and 'eyes that conveyed a thousand unspeakable thoughts', and somehow, millions of lonely women buy into this crap, because Barbara Cartland continues to be the biggest sellin' authoress of all time, even though she's currently deader than hell.

I've stared a million gals in the eye, and they've always stared back. That's 'cause *they were backed into a corner.* Any anthropologist will tell you the reason creatures stare at each other is to ward off imminent attack. Starin' into someone's eyes *demands* a response of some kind.

That person will either stare back, look away, or smile.

If he or she stares back, they're bein' defensive. If they look away, it means they don't give a shit. But if they *smile*, well, you assume it's attraction, and you're on your way to the Mattress Races don't you? Of course you do, *because that's always how it happens in beer ads and Barbara Cartlandland.*

But that ain't necessarily what's going on. Nothin' is more misleadin' than a smile. It is the surest sign that you are dealin' with a slippery individual. Who smiles a lot? Politicians, car salesmen, Jesus freaks, daytime chat-show hosts, clowns, Prozac addicts, flight attendants, pot heads. A smile is supposed to be disarmin'. Why would you let someone disarm you?

If you look into a stranger's eyes and they smile at you, it means one of two things. Either they're nervous, or they feel cornered. Either way, what they are doin', essentially, is barin' their teeth, same as chimps when confronted by a superior. What it means is you've overstepped your boundaries and they're just tryin' to survive your intrusive introduction.

And that's what a 'lingering gaze' is. A form of defense. Of course you don't want to hear this. You *want* to believe in romantic fiction. You don't want the dry, scientific truth: that Darwin and Mead and all those other anthropologists had more of an understandin' of romance than some purple pandering pimpmistress like Barbara Cartland ever did. Darwin would've probably sold a hell of a lot more anthropology books if he'd put some bare-chested, horse-bound stud on the cover instead of that chimp-to-man conga line you usually see.

It ain't possible to look into someone's eyes and see their 'soul'. No one, except clairvoyants and ghost hunters can see souls and frankly, if I saw a soul, I'd be scared shitless. What you will see are pupils, and if they're slightly dilated, that *might* be an indication of interest. But it's more likely a sign of inebriation.

In other words, *the eyes always play their cards close to the chest.* And *that's* where you oughta be looking. The chest.

Again, you gotta defer to Darwin on this one. All male species, when they're attracted to a female, inflate themselves. It happens in snakes, it happens in toads, it happens in pigeons and it happens in men. They *make* themselves bigger. They puff out their chests, straighten their spine, try to look like they could single-handedly lift a tractor if it fell on you by accident. *This* is the initial sign of male attraction. Watch a man in a bar when a good-lookin' gal approaches him. He looks like an airbag coming out of a steerin' wheel.

Women don't really need to inflate themselves. Nature's already done that for them. But if a gal is attracted to you, the first thing she'll do is arch her back. Like a wary cat. Sure, there'll be the attendant flickin' of hair, maybe a slight raise of the eyebrow, a tilt of the head, but the *real* giveaway is the arched back – which thrusts those little spacehoppers of hers ever so slightly forward, signifyin' openness. That's what two people should look for when they meet – swellin' and inflammation.

The truest sign of Romance – now, pay attention here – is synchronicity. When two people are genuinely attracted to each other, unwittingly, they start to ape each other's movements. He crosses his legs, she crosses hers. He touches his ear, she touches hers. That's the real indication of sparks.

One of my favorite bars of all time is called Shifty's Saloon. Shifty's is out on Tennessee 247, west of Knoxville. It has a big neon sign outside that says, 'Liquor in the Front, Poker in the Rear'. It also boasts The Biggest Horseshoe Bar East of the Mississippi.

If you don't know what a horseshoe bar is, lemme explain.

81

Someone came up with the idea a while back that if a bar was horseshoe-shaped, the patrons would make more eye contact with each other, which would lead to more socializing and, ultimately, more romance.

As a social experiment, I have to say it was a partial success. I made some good acquaintances in there. What I found particularly engagin' about the horseshoe bar was because of the distance – too far away from the person on the other side to actually talk to them – I had to rely on gestures. I'd look across that bar, see someone and smile. They'd smile back. I'd raise my glass in acknowledgement and they'd raise their glass. I'd sway to a Merle Haggard song on the jukebox – they'd sway along as well. There was a fantastic silent movie going on here. Not a word of conversation was ever exchanged. So what you had there was pure synchronicity. It was primitive and mysterious and damned sexy and, more often than not, I'd get up, slip on my jacket, they'd slip on theirs, and we'd head out to my truck.

Except when I got outside, there was only me. That's because *I'd actually been looking in a mirror at myself.* Shifty tore that old horseshoe bar out years ago because it was leadin' to too many staredowns and fistfights. But like I said, there was definitely some synchronicity going on there and I felt it.

IN THE FEDERAL COURTHOUSE OF TENNESSEE AT KNOXVILLE, TENNESSEE

Otis Lee Crenshaw vs. Crazy David Designs, Inc.

Presiding Judge: Hon. Howard Murtaugh. Federal Court, District 3, Knoxville, Tennessee

Plaintiff: David Beltrano, President and Owner of Crazy David Designs Inc., San Diego, California

Plaintiff Representative: Thomas B. Scheckler, Attorney. Scheckler, Scheckler and Scheckler, San Diego, California

Defendant: Otis Lee Crenshaw, no current address

Defendant Representative: Mr Crenshaw chooses to represent himself

OFFICIAL TRIAL TRANSCRIPT

JUDGE MURTAUGH: Mr Crenshaw, this is a respected court of law. You are wearing a sleeveless T-shirt in my courtroom.

OTIS LEE CRENSHAW: Yeah? So?

JUDGE MURTAUGH: I suggest you find more appropriate attire before we continue with this trial.

OTIS LEE CRENSHAW: Far's I'm concerned, this is appropriate attire. Hell, the trial's about T-shirts ain't it?

JUDGE MURTAUGH: Find something to cover your arms or I'll hold you in contempt of court.

[*Pause in proceedings while Mr Crenshaw borrows a jacket from someone in visitors' area.*]

OTIS LEE CRENSHAW: You happy?

JUDGE MURTAUGH: You may proceed to question the plaintiff.

OTIS LEE CRENSHAW: Uh, right, okay. For the record, would you state your name?

DAVID BELTRANO: David Beltrano.

OTIS LEE CRENSHAW: 'Scuse me, but ain't it 'Crazy' David Beltrano?

DAVID BELTRANO: Well, that's the name of my company.

OTIS LEE CRENSHAW: And do you answer to the name 'Crazy' David?

DAVID BELTRANO: Sure. On occasion, someone will ask me if I'm 'Crazy' David, the T-shirt guy.

OTIS LEE CRENSHAW: And you answer yes?

DAVID BELTRANO: Yeah.

OTIS LEE CRENSHAW: So you admit you're crazy, David?

REP. SCHECKLER: Objection, Your Honor.

OTIS LEE CRENSHAW: Judge, I would like to move for a mistrial on grounds of insanity.

JUDGE MURTAUGH: What?

84

OTIS LEE CRENSHAW: He just admitted he's crazy. You heard him.

JUDGE MURTAUGH: May I remind you the plaintiff is not on trial here. You are. Also, you will refer to me as 'Your Honor', not 'Judge'.

OTIS LEE CRENSHAW: Alright, alright. So, 'Crazy' David. You make novelty T-shirts, correct?

DAVID BELTRANO: Correct.

OTIS LEE CRENSHAW: And one of your most popular designs is the two ducks fucking?

JUDGE MURTAUGH: Mr Crenshaw. You will refrain from use of that word in my courtroom.

OTIS LEE CRENSHAW: Alright, fornicating ducks. You sell a lot of fornicating ducks, right?

DAVID BELTRANO: We do alright with that one.

OTIS LEE CRENSHAW: And did you get permission from United Airlines to use their logo?

REP. SCHECKLER: Objection, Your Honor. That's irrelevant.

JUDGE MURTAUGH: Overruled. Answer the question.

DAVID BELTRANO: No. I didn't. The design is clearly a parody of a well-known trademark. I own the design and it can't be recreated without licensed consent. You were not consented to display my design on your truck.

OTIS LEE CRENSHAW: Do you advertise these shirts?

DAVID BELTRANO: Yes, we advertise in a few publications. Surfer magazines, skateboard magazines.

OTIS LEE CRENSHAW: But your best advertisement is the design itself, right?

DAVID BELTRANO: What do you mean?

OTIS LEE CRENSHAW: I mean, people see someone wearing the fornicating-ducks T-shirt and decide they want one for themselves, right?

DAVID BELTRANO: I suppose so, yes.

OTIS LEE CRENSHAW: So, if I'm displaying your logo on the side of my truck, ain't that actually free advertising for your T-shirts?

REP. SCHECKLER: Objection, Your Honor. The nature of advertisements is irrelevant.

OTIS LEE CRENSHAW: I'm doing you a favor, ain't I, 'Demented' David?

REP. SCHECKLER: Objection. Your Honor, will you ask him to stop insinuating my client is mentally handicapped?

JUDGE MURTAUGH: Objection sustained. Follow another line of reasoning, Mr Crenshaw. And stop baiting the witness with the wrong adjective.

OTIS LEE CRENSHAW: May I go on record as sayin' this is not the witness I requested. You will note my affidavit that specifically requested I would like to talk to Willie Nelson or the guy who plays harmonica for Willie Nelson or Cindy Crawford because, frankly, this guy is a tool.

REP. SCHECKLER: Objection.

JUDGE MURTAUGH: Sustained. One more outburst like that Mr Crenshaw and . . .

OTIS LEE CRENSHAW: Sorry. Your Honor, can I approach the bench?

JUDGE MURTAUGH: What is it?

OTIS LEE CRENSHAW: How'm I doin' so far?

JUDGE MURTAUGH: Mr Crenshaw, I advised you prior to this hearing that you were making a big mistake representing yourself.

OTIS LEE CRENSHAW: So it's unwise?

JUDGE MURTAUGH: It's downright stupid.

OTIS LEE CRENSHAW: Aha! Hear that, everyone? The judge proclaimed me stupid. Your Honor, can I remove this jacket for a second?

JUDGE MURTAUGH: Why?

OTIS LEE CRENSHAW: I wanna show you something. [*Removes jacket, turns his back to judge.*] What's it say on the back of this T-shirt?

JUDGE MURTAUGH: It says 'I'M STUPID'. And you are. Now put your jacket back on.

OTIS LEE CRENSHAW: Ask 'Nutcake' David here what his biggest-selling design is. Ain't it the combination 'I'M STUPID', 'I'M WITH STUPID' his 'n' hers ensemble?

DAVID BELTRANO: Yes, that's our biggest seller.

OTIS LEE CRENSHAW: And you own that?

DAVID BELTRANO: Yes. It was my idea.

OTIS LEE CRENSHAW: So no one is allowed to proclaim they're stupid without getting permission from you?

REP. SCHECKLER: Objection, Your Honor.

OTIS LEE CRENSHAW: Because the Judge just pronounced me stupid. So the Judge just infringed on your copyright. So far as I'm concerned, he's as fuckin' guilty as I am.

JUDGE MURTAUGH: You are in contempt of this court.

Gold Wing Days

In the Unit, you ain't allowed to have any pictures of your wife or girlfriend, but you *are* allowed all the girlie mags you can get your hands on.

These are the kind of pointless, humiliating rules you get used to. The worst thing about the Unit is paralytic boredom, followed closely by loneliness. I fought off boredom by learnin' the piano. But loneliness was a motherfucker.

Contrary to what you've heard, not all prisons are crawling with predatory homosexuals. The overdone joke is, 'Hey, don't drop the soap!' To me, that joke implies homosexuals are kind of lazy, or can't control their urges and, consequently, will park themselves in any convenient orifice. Maybe that goes on at hardcore places like Folsom or Marion but at Brushy Mountain, as far as carefree, random sodomy goes, we were a fairly genteel bunch. Furtive inquiries got you lined out quick. Still, to be safe, I gave myself a tattoo. A woman's name on your arm goes a long way toward avoidin' uncomfortable associations in prison. One night, I borrowed some printer's ink from a cellmate and filed the end of a Bic pen to make perforations in my skin. There's only been three women in my life that meant anything to me. There was my first wife, Brenda, who'd wanted somethin' more than I could give her. There was Brenda #2, who'd only wanted back what I'd taken from her. And there was my momma, The Supreme Brenda, who'd traded what she could never have for somethin' she never needed, namely my Old Man. In my mind, the three of them formed an unholy alliance and so that's the name I carved on to my arm, knowin' full well as I did that I was narrowin' any future romantic prospects. From hereon in, it was Brendas or nothin'. I saw myself from that point on as a purist.

Most of the talk at Brushy concerned sexual prowess. Who could bang the most. Who could bang the longest. Who could bang the drunkest. Who could bang the loudest. Who's paid the most for a whore. Who's paid the least for a whore. Who wouldn't go near a whore, not even if they was being *pushed*. Who's stood up in it. Who's knocked it out of the frame. I'd sit in my cell and hear someone rifflin' through *Hustler*, practically fuming over the pictures with disdain, as if *these* women were beneath *them*.

'Ah hell, they've touched these photos up. Ain't nothin' in nature that pink. Except a flamingo.'

That was Mama Herk. Mama was a Coke-machine-sized black ex-club bouncer who was doing three years for holding up a White Hen Pantry convenience store with a ten-pound bag of ice. He had gotten the Korean owner on the floor and was threatenin' to crush his head with the ice when two cops came in, drew their guns, then waited until the ice was sufficiently melted before movin' in. Mama was in the cell two up from me.

'Know why flamingoes are pink?' I called, hopin' to draw him into a civil conversation. Nature, famous civil-war battles, baseball. Anything but pussy.

'No. Why are flamingos pink?'

90

'Cause they eat pink algae.'

There was a long silence.

Then Mama called out, 'Hear that sound, Crenshaw?'

'What sound?' I didn't hear nothin'.

'Exactly. That's the sound of no one givin' a shit.'

Suddenly from another cell, a voice joined in.

'I used to bang a truck-stop waitress named Alga.'

That'd be Leech. Leech was in for industrial theft – caught tryin' to remove a segment of copper roofing from the Knoxville Library.

'Had a cat like an old man's wallet.'

And now there was no turnin' back. Voice after voice would join in.

'Oh man, that's a heartbreaker. If it ain't tight, it ain't right.'

'Ah hell, it's all the same upside down!'

'That ain't true.'

'The hell it ain't.'

'My gal's done shaved off a corner of snatch hair and has a tiny tattoo of a little guy pushin' a lawn mower. If I'm lyin', I'm dyin'!'

Mornin' till night, that's how it went. Same subject, new adjective: youngest, oldest, darkest, pinkest, smallest, tightest, most fragrant, skankiest, stingiest, most accommodating . . . *pussy, pussy, pussy. Hustler* and *Penthouse* and all the other porn rags had reduced these men to obsessive precisionists.

After a few months of this shit I was about to go full-tilt loco.

I put in a request to see the chaplain.

A few days later, two Corrections Officers showed up at my cell and marched me to his office. They left us alone, but I knew they were right outside the door. Most COs don't think

91

too much of chaplains. They refer to them as 'crutches'. They think the chaplain gets too close with the inmates, too personal. COs don't believe in gettin' personal with inmates. And the inmates don't get personal with the COs. The chaplain always gets caught in the middle, 'cause he's staff and doesn't want the COs comin' down on him. But how do you deal with inmates' problems without gettin' personal? Chaplains must feel like they're in way over their heads, like a boy-scout leader sent into Nam.

I took a seat across from the chaplain's desk. He seemed like an OK guy, cautious and scholarly. He wore an old-fashioned string tie that somehow put me at ease.

'Is this a confidential discussion?' I said.

'To a degree,' the chaplain replied. 'What's bothering you?'

'What's botherin' me, Father, is it's pussy this, pussy that all day long around here. You know what I mean?'

His lip fluttered.

'I'm not sure.'

'The conversations around here. "Who's had the youngest, who's had the oldest, who's had the tightest, who's had the floppiest . . ." This morning I had to sit there and listen to a discussion about the *clumsiest* pussy anyone's ever encountered. I don't even know how *that* got started.'

The chaplain blanched but I kept goin'. 'The way I see it, these men have long forgotten there's any other *part* of a woman. A face, for instance. And I sure as hell don't wanna end up like these sad sonofabitches.'

I sensed the chaplain was about to launch into some kind of Keeping the Faith peptalk, but I cut him off.

'Now I been thinkin'. We ain't allowed no pictures of wives or girlfriends in here, and that's downright inhumane.'

'I agree,' said the chaplain.

92

'But if those wives or girlfriends showed up in *Hustler*, well the men *would* have pictures of 'em, right?'

'*Hustler*?' the chaplain said. 'As in *nude*?'

'Well yeah, as in nude. But it's their wives. I mean it's not really porn if you actually care about the woman in the picture, right?'

'Porn isn't my field of expertise,' said the chaplain.

'I understand that. But, supposin' – just supposin' – you were to contact someone like, I don't know, Larry Flynt and ask if he'd be interested?'

'Interested in what?'

'A photo spread. "Girlfriends and Wives of Brushy Mountain Prison".'

'You want me to write to Larry Flynt?'

'Yeah!'

'I'm a clergyman, not a pimp.'

'Exactly. Larry Flynt's always claimin' to be a born-again Christian. Ever since he got shot in the ass, anyway. You write him and explain the situation here – that men can't even wake up in the mornin' to a picture of someone they care about. He'll *jump* on the idea.'

The chaplain massaged the bridge of his nose. 'I have a hard time believing you're concerned about the comfort of other men in the Unit,' he said.

'I'm concerned about my own comfort!' I said. 'I can't take any more of this pussy yammering! And yeah, I'm workin' my own angle on this thing, but you ain't gotta be concerned with that.'

The chaplain shifted uneasily. I was hopin' he wasn't gonna snitch me out to the Chief CO or the warden. He eyeballed me for a moment, then said, 'What's in it for me?'

Jesus, *everyone* in the Unit had an angle.

'What are you lookin' for?' I asked.

'Would you consider givin' your soul to the Lord?'

I should have seen that comin'. I'll bet the COs standin' mainline right outside the door were laughin' their asses off. How many times had they seen some fresh convert come glidin' out of the chaplain's office thinkin' the Lord had just reduced his sentence? Allegedly, the parole board gave special consideration to inmates who had 'found the Lord'. But far as I was concerned, the Lord didn't factor into it much. It's just the religious guys behaved better so they ended up with more Good Time. I'm bettin' God knows exactly how ropy a prison Christian is. As soon as they get out they ain't gonna be playin' for his team no more.

'I don't know,' I said. 'I ain't quite ready to shake hands with the J man. But if you were to write Larry Flynt, who knows? I might come around.'

'Let me think about it,' he said.

I ended up doin' chapel detail for ninety cents an hour. On Sunday mornings I would put out foldin' chairs and mimeographed hymn sheets. There were four different services, beginnin' with the Methodists at 10 a.m., then the AME Zionists, then the Pentecostalists, then the Baptists at 6 p.m. It was breezy work and usually there was an hour or so between services, so I would go over and chink around on the upright Baldwin in the corner. I didn't even know what I was doin' – I figured out chords pretty much from scratch, but I was thinkin' maybe I ought to try writin' some songs. I would sit in my cell during the week, write lyrics, then on Sundays sit down at the piano and try to put some kind of tune around 'em. It didn't occur to me that this was the beginnin' of my stellar country music career, and if anybody had told me I'd one day be making a livin' as a musician, I'd have laughed and said they weren't right in the head.

*　　*　　*

Three months later – prison time moves glacially – the chaplain called me into his office and said Larry Flynt hadn't bothered to reply, but he'd found a bikers' magazine who'd agreed to run the photos.

'Fuckin' fantastic!' I said. Harleys *and* naked babes. The men would go apeshit.

'Which magazine is it, *Easyriders*?' I asked.

'No . . . *Gold Wing Gals*,' the chaplain replied.

Gold Wing Gals! I'd never heard of it. I knew Gold Wings were big, tricked-out Hondas. And Hondas ain't Harleys, that's for sure. Still, who cared what kind of bike it was if your girlfriend was draped over it, gloriously naked?

It got better. The chaplain said *Gold Wing Gals* would pay fifty dollars for each photo. If I could get them a list of girls, they would arrange to bring them into a studio, shoot a full session and run the best pictures.

Now I had a decent scam goin'. I went back to my wing and dropped the word about the photo spread. If your gal's so fuckin' hot, I said, put your money where your mouth is. Each man who could persuade his girl to pose would have to pay me two cartons of cigarettes, else she didn't get on the list. By the end of the week, I had thirty-five takers.

I explained to the men they needed to write to their gals and convince them to go for it – which should have been a breeze. I didn't realize half the men at Brushy Mountain were functional illiterates who could barely compose a ransom note, much less a letter.

In the end *I* had to compose a form letter and get them to sign it:

Dear (name of wife or girlfriend)
   I miss you and long for your face. Sadly, it's fading

from my memory because the Tennessee Department of Corrections won't even let a man wake up to a photo of his gal. So could you please go to the address below, climb on a bike (naked) and collect your fifty bucks?

Lovingly,
(name of inmate)

The letters would all have to go through the chaplain or else they would have never gotten past the censors. It took another two months to gather all the replies, but eventually the chaplain had a list of eight wives, thirteen girlfriends and one inmate's mom to pose naked for *Gold Wing Gals*.

That's how I managed to establish myself as some kind of shaker at Brushy Mountain. In prison, you've got no credence until you got some kind of racket going. Hooch, dope, protection, gamblin', AA batteries, porn mags, moonpies, Snickers bars, scrabble tournaments, even the nightly viewin' schedule in the TV lounge. If there's an activity, someone's tradin' on it. You see six guys whilin' away the afternoon shootin' hoops in the exercise yard, someone's runnin' a book on it.

Of course, once you have a racket goin', the inmates *completely* distrust you 'cause there's no such thing as an honest racket. But at least they know where you're comin' from. It's the guys who keep to themselves and just do their time who make cons suspicious.

The conversations on the wing shifted from nondescript pussy to whose wife, or girlfriend (or mom) was going to turn out the hottest in the spread. The idle bravado of guys like Mama Herk and Leech didn't carry much weight anymore. If you had a Gold Wing Gal in the runnin', you were the new kingpin. The bettin' slips started flying. Me, I sat in my cell, wrote lyrics and smoked like a fiend.

The first song that I would really call a *song*, I wrote one night when I was blue, reflectin' on almost every woman and drink I'd ever known. It was pretty much a crawl-inside-the-bottle-and-die song, so that's what I called it:

You got a knack, baby, make a man feel about
    three inches high
I don't know why, I don't know why
But I shrink a little, every time you tell a lie
I'm gonna crawl inside a bottle
I'm gonna crawl inside a bottle
I'm goin' to crawl inside a bottle and die.

When you look down that rim, you'll say, 'Oh my
    God, it's him'
Well once I was a rebel, now I'm the size of a
    pebble
So I'm goin' to crawl inside a bottle and die

I'll be down here with the drips, not far from your
    lyin' lips
You're gonna put me on a shelf. Fine, I'll immerse
    myself
But I wish I had a gin, for all the nights I said,
    'Hey where you been?'
I wish I had a Scotch, for all the nights I spent
    checkin' my watch
I wish I had a shot of Old Grand-Dad, for the
    night you spent with
My Old Grand-Dad

You gonna put me on a shelf. Fine, I'll immerse
   myself.
Hey, watch me wiggle, watch me squirm
Hello tequila worm
I'm goin' to crawl inside a bottle and die.

Hell, as far as I was concerned, that song was as good as anything I'd ever heard come out of the radio. *And* it was honest.
I made up my mind to try it out in front of an audience.

   Anyone who tells you Maximum Security prison ain't
nerve-racking is lyin'. There's a thousand things that can
happen to you, you never see comin'. Someone can slip into
your cell when you're dead asleep, throw a blanket over
your head and start smackin' you with a pillowcase full of
AA batteries. The COs can roust you for a search, bangin'
on your cell bars with hammers and belt buckles, rattlin'
you out of your reverie. The squawk of two dozen different radios and tape decks all goin' at once makes your skin
feel like sandpaper. Then when it quiets down you wonder
if the reason the music's stopped is because someone's gathered up all the batteries . . .

   You walk down hallways practically fuckin' pirouetting.
Anyone could be behind you. You're nervous in the shower.
You're nervous in the TV room. You're nervous shooting
hoops in the rec yard. You know that feeling you get when
you lean back too far in a chair and lose your balance, and
then catch yourself just in time? In prison, that's how you
feel *all* the time.

   But I'll tell you this. None of that was as unsettling as
the idea of performin' a song in front of people.

The followin' Sunday, I prepped the service as quick as I
could. Then I sat down at that Baldwin and ran through
'Crawl Inside a Bottle' about twenty times, throwin' in all

the chords I knew and makin' up a couple that don't exist. When the Methodists straggled in, all six of them, I asked the minister if I could play a hymn on the piano. He said 'be my guest' and halfway through the service, I made my country and western debut.

I sat down at the piano, feelin' like I was underwater. My fingers were shakin' so much I kept hittin' the wrong keys and the song started out like some kind of mutant jitterbug theme for a St Vitus dance. Then I couldn't get my voice to come out the way it did when I sang on my own. I was mumbly and tense and ended up half speakin', half singin'. But when it was over I got a few appreciative nods from the inmates, and I reckon had it been anywhere but church, they might have applauded. The minister thanked me and I went to the back and took a seat, shakin', but weirdly elated. I'll never forget that feelin' as long as I live. Every corpuscle in my body felt wired. By God, I was a *songwriter*.

'Crawl Inside a Bible and Die . . .' the minister said, beginning his sermon. 'Otis's words could not be any truer . . .'

What the hell was he talkin' about!? I hadn't mentioned nothin' about crawlin' inside a Bible! All through the sermon he kept referring to my song, sayin' we all have to crawl inside the Bible and die to be reborn again.

This was my first searing lesson in how misunderstood an artist can sometimes be.

I played the song three more times that day and every damned congregation was convinced I was singin' *Bible*, not *bottle*. The rumor got out around the wing that I'd found Jesus, gotten all pious and now I was gonna nix the whole *Gold Wing Gal* scheme. My reputation was on the ropes. Everyone stopped talkin' to me, except for the Baptists and Pentecostalists who started skulking around my cell wantin' me to 'witness' with them. It was hell six ways from Sunday.

Man, did I need that *Gold Wing Gals* spread to come out soon.

In prison, cigarettes are currency and, like any currency, someone is always tryin' to figure out novel new ways of gettin' their hands on them. Among inmates, there's two ways of rippin' each other off. There's the artless way, where you just take what you want from someone and see if they'll stand up to you. Some new lop shows up and within days someone's stolen his smokes. If he doesn't say anything about it, you know he's just some punk. Then the guy who stole the cigarettes shows up at his cell and says, 'Hey, I hear someone stole your smokes. I know who it is and I can get 'em back for you. But you and me are gonna enter a partnership. You're gonna do my laundry. Get me anything I want from the commissary. And in return, I'm gonna make sure no one touches you. Deal?'

Now the kid ain't that stupid. He knows this is the dude who stole his cigarettes, but he doesn't want any trouble. So he says 'yeah' and now he's owned. But eventually the lop is going to get fed up with the idea of bein' bought and paid for, and he's gonna pay someone *else* his cigarettes to go around at night, throw a blanket over the other guy's head and smack him with a pillowcase full of AA batteries. Now, there might be some kind of lesson about revenge and self-preservation in that story, but that ain't the point. The point is, any way you look at it, the kid is out a lot of cigarettes.

Then there's the artful way of acquiring cigs, like my Gold Wing scam. The reason it was artful was because I was able to hang on to them long enough to smoke every last one.

As much as I tried to convince the other cons the photo spread was still on, I knew some weren't buyin' it. I began to think I was marked for an AA raid.

You can always spot the guy in prison who knows some-one's got it in for him. He'll sit on the john with one leg out of his pants, just in case he has to get away fast. Two guys come barging in on him with a bag of batteries, and his pants are down around his ankles, he ain't going far. So he keeps one foot free for mobility. But it's a sure sign he's scared.

Me, I kept both feet in my pants. I didn't want anyone who saw me sitting on the crapper to think I was scared. Hell, if you don't have your dignity in prison, what *do* you have?

I'd been sentenced to eighteen months for stealin' trailers. I'd done almost nine of 'em when I got a letter whisked into my cell one afternoon:

> In response to the pleas of your lawyers for a more lenient decision, this commission has considered your institutional behavior and achievements, and deemed it sufficient to release you to community service begin-ning immediately.
>
> The Warden
> Brushy Mountain State Correctional Facility

Two hours later, two COs showed up at my cell.

'Pack your shit, Crenshaw,' one of them said. 'You're being turned out.'

I was already packed. I had a toothbrush, a razor and a sheath full of unfinished songs.

The COs led me along the wing and I could feel seething fury from the inmates who thought I'd ripped them off. I stopped by the chaplain's office. I wanted to say goodbye and inform him that he could have my soul now, because my ass was headin' down the road! I waltzed into his office and damned if he wasn't leafin' through the new issue of *Gold Wing Gals*. Wouldn't you know it would arrive the same goddamned day I got released?

Of course I had a look. There were a dozen copies stacked on his desk. I picked one up and went right to 'Wives, Girlfriends and Moms of Brushy Mountain'.

The photos showed true quality. Attention had been paid to lightin' – both the bikes and the girls were captured flatteringly. The girls should have looked very alluring, straddlin' the Gold Wings or draped over the handlebars – every accessorist dream. But unlike the Harley owner's wind-through-the-hair approach to freedom ridin', the Gold Wing enthusiast is more of a stickler for safety. Which is why every girl in the spread was wearing a full-faced helmet. They looked like gumball machines with tits.

The chaplain shook my hand and wished me luck. I went straight to Processing, signed out and walked out of the main entrance to Brushy Mountain.

Then I married the first woman to come around the corner.

Brenda #3

'Stay out of trouble, Crenshaw.' That's the last thing they'd said to me.

Like everyone who's done time, I'd always viewed trouble as the consequence of doin' bad things. But now, I saw it as a commodity. I'd discovered that trouble creates dissatisfaction which creates inspiration which creates songs. What I *needed* was trouble.

I was tryin' to play down my elation at bein' out. I didn't trust happiness. At Brushy there were lots of prisoners on meds – paratroopers we called 'em – total goners. They couldn't deal with the reality of prison so they just floated, blissfully. And to me, they didn't look much different than the kind of balloon-faced idiots you see at a Barry Manilow concert. Hell, no one who's happy ever accomplished a goddamned significant thing. Look at Albert Einstein. Discovered his theory of relativity at twenty-eight. Why? Because he was tryin' to get into some Fräulein's pants! Because she said, 'I'll bang you the moment you can explain to me why the spokes on a wheel appear to be goin' backward when they're actually goin' forward.' Then he went and got himself happily married and never came close to another $E=MC^2$-type deal. Just sat around tootling on his saxophone and nailin' the wife all day. A one-hit wonder. Happiness kills testosterone. That ain't just me sayin' that – that's the medical truth and you can look it up. Once you've lost your testosterone, you're as useless as a bag of wet mice.

Goddamned America believes happiness is its birthright, just because that's what it says in the Declaration of Independence: 'Life, Liberty and Happiness'. But it doesn't. Read the fine print. It says 'the pursuit of happiness', which is an entirely different thing. *Pursuit* means 'good luck trying'. Well, fuck that for a game of soldiers. I'd rather have my testosterone.

I stopped at the junction with the Wartburg Highway, thinkin' I'd thumb into the Greyhound station. I spotted a house across the road and damned if it wasn't a whole warehouse of trouble: a battered-women's shelter.

The sign didn't actually say 'battered'. It said 'Harriet Tubman Women's Shelter'. But the house itself, a huge crumbling shipwreck with peeling sideboards and flimsy shutters, overgrown weeping willows and an unmowed yard, certainly fit the description of 'battered'. I figured the gals inside had bigger fish to fry than home repair and lawn management.

Most fellas would view a battered-women's shelter as a crate full of damaged goods. But, me, I stood there and imagined the plight of all those women inside – lovely creatures who'd all somehow managed to end up with the wrong man. Hell, every woman in there was probably ripe for affection, with just one minimum requirement: Don't Hit Me.

Right there at the side of the road a new song came to me. I'd taken to carryin' a pen and a few sheets of paper in my shirt pocket, for moments of musical inspiration. I sat down and scratched out a new future hit.

> Bright lights, barstools, evenings on the prowl
> Discos where the women look all right
> But I ain't gonna waste my time
> I was never good at any pickup lines
> So, I'm goin' down to the battered-women's shelter
> I'm goin' down to the battered-women's shelter
> I'm goin' down to the battered-women's shelter
> Gonna find me a woman
>
> Lucy's been here for a year or more
> Sandy claims she just walked into a door
> Sally's just stayin' till she finds a job
> Jody's on the run from the Russian mob
> Look out ladies, I'm no James Dean
> But every other man in your life's been mean
> So I'm goin' down to the battered-women's shelter
> I'm goin' down to the battered-women's shelter
> I'm goin' down to the battered-women's shelter
> Gonna find me a woman

I looked up from my writin' to see a gal in the side of the yard, pinning laundry to a clothesline, white haired, almond skinned, with startling gray eyes, like the one weird one you see on every Australian Shepherd. She looked like the kind of gal kids might call a 'Devil Woman', ancient and young at the same time. You coulda asked her to the dance or asked her what it was like in the Big War.

I thought she might be a Melungeon.

No one can explain where Melungeons originally came from or how they ended up in Tennessee. In fact, no one can

105

explain much of *anything* about them and if you ask around East Tennessee you'll get a one-word answer: inbred.

Now, I don't wanna get righteous here or anything, but 'inbred' is one of them terms that really puts a bug up my ass. I realize that Southerners are the first to use it on their own kind, but it's a cavalier description everywhere. Call someone an inbred and wait for everyone to laugh. Yeeha! We've all seen *Deliverance*.

'Nigger.' 'Spic.' 'Wop.' Those words are specific to racism, and the people who use them know you know where they stand on things. But callin' someone an inbred is an abuse of scientific terminology. Unless you're a geneticist, you don't know what the fuck you're talkin' about.

Melungeons are an ethnic mystery and they prefer to stay that way. Whatever oral history they own, they've kept to themselves. The most anyone really knows is they are equal parts white, black and olive. If that's inbred, then pay close attention. 'Cause when you see a Melungeon, you're lookin' into the future.

The only thing batterin' her at the moment was a strong mountain breeze, flutterin' her dress, whippin' her hair against her face and makin' the laundry flap around her like white flames. I couldn't decide if she looked troubled or troublesome.

I've never been shy about approachin' women, but when you see one outside a battered-women's shelter you know you got to be a little bit cautious, so I just kinda waved to her from across the road. The laundry was in her face and she never saw me.

Presently I heard a vehicle approachin'. I looked out to the highway but all I could see was an ungodly road construction project: a deranged array of amber lights, reflective strips, yellow and black caution hatches, a haywire antennae, all framed in an outline of small flutterin' American flags. What's more, the construction site seemed to be movin' toward me. I realized then it was a motorcycle – a Gold Wing, wouldn't you know. With Ohio plates. I thought to myself, 'Anyone lit up like this must be so paranoid about being hit he shouldn't be on a bike in the first place.'

Gradually, the rider eased the thing to a stop beside me. He wore a creamy leather jacket with lapels the size of Cadillac fins. His teeth were brown and contorted, like cracked pecans. He had a wind-burnished face, raw and tobacco-colored – a road veteran for sure. Both his jacket and helmet were covered entirely in what appeared to be tiny eagle-like insignias.

'Nice ride,' I called out, knowin' that's the greetin' any Gold Wing owner likes to hear. What I wanted to say was, 'Where's the fuckin' parade?'

'Where you headed?' he shouted over the chug of the engine.

'Bus station,' I said. He reached into the pannier and handed me a battered football helmet. The helmet had 'MASON HIGH SCHOOL FIGHTING MUSKRATS' written across it. Beneath the writin' was a small cartoon muskrat wearing a football helmet that read, with a view toward infinity: 'MASON HIGH SCHOOL FIGHTING MUSKRATS'. I slipped it over my head and climbed on behind him. I noticed then that the dull winged splotches all over him were dead bugs – moths, cicadas and a few trophy-sized crickets.

By the clothesline, the gal was still fightin' to keep her dress down.

'There's a real Daisy Mae,' he called over his shoulder. We eased back on to the highway, he floored the bike and I had to wrap my arms around a man, somethin' I'd just spent nine months avoidin'.

The bike was too loud for any conversation so I just

watched the countryside slip by. It was twilight and the warm wind reminded me of the prison laundry. Man it felt good to be free. We got to the Wartburg Bus Station and I gave him back the football helmet, thanked him and went inside. I didn't even know where I was headed. First bus anywhere, I reckon.

The woman behind the counter said there was a 2 a.m. to Memphis, then on to San Francisco. I wasn't allowed to leave the state but forty-five dollars would get me to Graceland. Fifty dollars was how much they'd given me when I got outta Brushy.

I went back outside and the fella was still there, sittin' broadside across the bike, blastin' *I Walk the Line* out of the bike's twin speakers. He had a sheet of sketch paper out and was makin' broad sweeps on it with a stick of charcoal. When I got close I could see it was my face. He looked up at me, sneezed violently, then launched into a fiery riposte to a question no one had asked.

'Johnny Cash!' he barked. 'The man is the Great Communicator! Think of the thousands of people arriving freshly to this country each day. It is as much as they can do to grasp anything of this huge confusing place and Johnny gives it to them in bite-sized chunks. I, for one, have not written the man off!' At that point his speech deteriorated into a volley of sneezes.

I waited until he'd cleared his chest of inhaled bugs. Then he shoved the sketch and the charcoal stick at me.

'Sign it to George Lively,' he said.

The sketch didn't look anything like me. At least I hoped it didn't. It looked as stiff and rudimentary as those art-school drawings in magazine ads. Anyway, I signed it and gave it back to him.

He studied the signature for a long time, then slipped the drawing into a vinyl, bug-covered sheath.

'Fresh outta Brushy are you, Otis Lee Crenshaw?' he said.

'What makes you say that?' I said.

'I recognize a prison tan. What were you in for?'

'Stealin' trailers.'

'Cargo?'

'No. Mobile homes.'

He thought about that one. Then he said, 'You lookin' to make some fast money or,' he indicated the music, 'more or less determined to Walk the Line?'

'I'm lookin' to catch my bus,' I said. 'But it ain't till 2 a.m. Why?'

'Let's go get us a cup of coffee,' he said.

George Lively needed a partner. We were sittin' in a coffee shop across from the bus station, full of cheery, sunken Tennessee faces. The menus were mimeographed and handwritten, and at the bottom the owners had mentioned they were glad for the comin' thunderstorms. I was diggin' into a matted pile of hash browns. Golden, crusty and fuckin' delicious, too. Christ Almighty, had I missed real cooking!

'You are familiar with the mighty TVA?' George asked.

'Somewhat,' I said. The TVA was the Tennessee Valley Authority, the big power company around these parts.

'While you've been in prison, the TVA has been very busy consolidating the power grid. A massive undertaking to say the least, and one that has provided a small windfall for the alert opportunist, such as yourself. Pass me the saccharine.'

He emptied the packet into his coffee and stirred it, shrouding himself over the cup like he was trying to heat his whole body. All around us, the suppertime locals chattered in vivacious, relaxed tones, their elbows hooked over the backs of the booths. It was weird to be back among

109

unthreatened diners. In prison everyone hunkered over their plates like a club owner counting the night's take.

'In all these little places,' George motioned out the window in the general direction of Wartburg, 'they're pulling down the insulated copper electrical wire and replacing it with CopperWeld.'

'CopperWeld?'

'Steel wire with just enough copper in it to act as a conductor. It's manufactured down in Mexico. The TVA is saving itself millions of dollars. These savings are not, as a rule, being passed on to users but rather are lining the pockets of various TVA Brahmins. How do you feel about that?'

'I can't change the world,' I said. 'I ain't a folk singer. But I'm thinkin' I got five dollars in my pocket and I am seriously considerin' goin' across the street to a bookstore and purchasin' a *Roget's Thesaurus*, a gift from me to you. In it, you'll find big words like 'Brahmin', and the equivalent *plain* words that *plain* guys like me understand.'

George studied me for a few moments. He carefully poured milk into his coffee from a novelty cow mug. You tipped the cow's mouth and it regurgitated milk. You could buy them for a dollar at the checkout counter.

I was waitin' for George to finish his coffee and pick up my bill so I could go back to the bus station and sit. I didn't much like anyone who knew more words than me. On the wall above the sit-down counter was a wooden sign featurin' the most concise joke I'd ever seen:

> FUNEM?
> SVFM
> FUNEX?
> SVFX
> OKILFMNX

'I'll tell you what,' George finally said.

'What?'

'Reason I got that Gold Wing, I can see everything. I drive up and down these roads and I study the power lines. Now what do you think I'm lookin' for?'

'I don't know, Glen Campbell?'

'Birds. Or rather, the absence of birds. A flock of birds will perch on insulated copper. But they won't perch on CopperWeld. They don't like the vibrations. So when I see a power line void of birds, I know there's a big pile of old copper nearby.'

He looked out the window at the street. 'And I tell you what.'

'What?'

'I ain't seen no goddamn birds around here. When the old wire comes down, they just wrap it in bundles and throw it on to a pile. It's just sitting there for the taking.'

'Sittin' where?'

'In the equipment yard of the Rural Electric Association.'

I thought about Leech, the guy on my wing doing a deuce for tryin' to steal a copper roof.

'How much is copper worth?' I said.

'Two dollars twelve a pound, any scrapyard. No questions asked neither.'

'You want me to help you steal copper?'

'Well, I realize it ain't as lofty an undertaking as mobile homes, but then . . . if you didn't need money, you wouldn't be riding the dog, would you?'

'What do we have to do?'

'You got to climb over a fence.'

'Ain't there a night watchman?' I asked.

'No. I already checked it out. Drove over there last night. It ain't even all that lit up.'

'What do we do, drape it over our shoulders?'

111

'I got a custom three-hundred-pound capacity bike trailer.'

'I got to think about this,' I said.

'Take your time,' said George.

A waitress, who had been keepin' a vigilant eye on diminished caffeine levels, appeared and poured us more coffee. I smiled at her, thrilled to be back in the world of thank-yous. I'd calculated, from studyin' the haircuts in the room, that there was one barber and one female stylist in Wartburg. What in the hell was it that resigned small-town women to a uniform broccoli patch of hair? The White-Haired Gal's was the only unfried hair I'd seen all day. I wondered if whoever had hit her resented nonconformity.

'As for the word "steal",' George said, 'you get to my age, you realize certain things promised you are not forthcoming. I served my country during Vietnam. It cost me my hip.'

He whipped his bug-infested jacket aside, and thrust the waistband of his pants downward, revealin' a scar like seams on a softball.

'Christ, you got that in Nam?'

'I never said I got it in Nam. I said I got it during Nam.'

He smacked his knuckles hard against the scar.

'Hear that? That's a plastic hip. Sounds like someone at the door, don't it?' He had raised himself half above the table to give any curious diners a good look. 'When I went into the service they was all made of metal. By the time I got out, they'd gone polyethylene. At the VA hospital, going under, I watched 'em pull it out of a box. Bone, stem and socket. Shining new. It said "Made in Hong Kong" on the box'.

'How's it workin'?' I asked

'Sixty percent mobility in my left leg. The VA considered that a fair enough return for my efforts to stem the flow of

Communism in south-east Asia. They cut off my benefits.'

'Assholes.'

'Assholes is right. I tell you what.'

'What?'

'My days as a champion figure skater are over!' He spluttered a violent laugh at himself that seemed to catch his lungs by surprise. Suddenly he collapsed into another sneezing fit. I got the feeling the man was slowly dismantling.

'You alright?' I asked.

'Fair amount of bugs this time of year,' he said. No shit. Every flyin' insect in the South was probably attracted to that Broadway Production he was ridin'. I waited while he sneezed up another spray of bug confetti, bits of which landed on the table. He examined them closely for a moment, then, lookin' fairly satisfied with the yield, took a drink of coffee.

'Why don't you wear a face shield?' I suggested.

'I like the wind in my face,' he replied. 'You wanna steal some copper or not?'

I went back to the bus station, cashed in my ticket and we rode out to a campground where George had pitched a small tent. I sat at a picnic table drinkin' from a bottle of Old Grand-Dad and watched him load the trailer: a flashlight, two pairs of work gloves, a thick canvas-backed sleeping bag, a sketch-book, a pack of charcoal pencils, and, for reasons I can only guess were sentimental, a giant laboratory jar containin' his original hip.

When he was done, he took a seat beside me, swigged the bourbon and instructed me what to do when I got inside the REA (Rural Electric Association) yard.

'I'll drape my sleeping bag over the top of the fence. That'll keep the barbed wire from nipping you. When you get inside, look for big stacks of insulated coil. If you check the end, you'll see the copper sticking out. Each coil weighs maybe fifty pounds. Drag 'em over to where I'll be waitin' on the other side of the fence and stack 'em there.'

'Right,' I said. It sounded easier than stealin' mobile homes.

'When I say we've got enough, we've got enough. Then you throw 'em over and I'll load 'em in the trailer,' George said. 'Don't get greedy. The trailer can only handle so much.'

We set off around midnight. The REA was about two miles out of town, back in the direction I'd come from. We passed the turn-off to Brushy and I got a little twinge of jitters. I couldn't imagine the split between George and me comin' to more than a few hundred bucks apiece, so that prison up the road was loomin' pretty large. Imagine havin' to admit to Leech I was back in for stealin' a goddamn coil of copper. Compared to his roof, where would that put me in the pecking order?

We pulled up at the REA, a squat white buildin' with a dancin' skeleton painted on the side. It had a light bulb head and lightnin' bolt body, the friendly face of Tennessee electricity. Behind the buildin' was an eight-foot chain-link fence and beyond that a yard full of hulking transformers and utility trucks.

George killed the lights on the Gold Wing and we sat there waitin': for barkin' dogs, lights comin' on, cars comin' up the highway. There's a perfect moment of stillness that thieves instinctively know is the right moment to move. I pulled on the work gloves and felt my old friend, adrenaline, course through me and, I had to admit, it was fuckin' sexy. Every time I'm about to do somethin' dangerous, an image of the last good-lookin' gal I've run across comes into my head. Don't ask me why. Maybe it's just a way of conjurin' up a patron saint, a good-luck charm, but when I went over the fence, I was thinkin' about the White-Haired Devil Woman.

There were only a few sodium lights on. They cast broad, menacing shadows off the transformers, vicious lookin' gray cylinders with ceramic capacitors on each side, like severed arms. I crawled over a stack of power poles and felt them turn under my feet. It would have been easy to get my fingers crushed in between them. Creosote stuck to my clothes – my only clothes. I had a vision of me in a laundromat, wearin' a garbage bag.

Next to a small shed, I found the copper. Damned if there wasn't a mountain of it. Hell, we weren't even gonna make a dent! I grabbed a fat, springy bale and dragged it across the yard. When I got to the fence, George was sittin' on his bike facin' the road. He had his sketch-pad out.

'What are you doing?' I whispered.

'Sketching the landscape.'

'At night?'

'It's my preferred medium. If a cop pulls in . . . "*Just drawin', Officer.*"'

I made seven more trips to the pile. George said, 'That'll do,' and I began hoistin' the bales over the fence. He dragged them over to the trailer, cursin' and hobblin' and gurglin' under his breath. I wondered if his Hong Kong hip was up for the task.

'You alright?' I said.

'Yeah. Hustle it now,' he grunted back.

I got the last coil across and shimmied back over the fence. George had stacked them into the trailer, which was now sinkin' over its own wheels. I pulled off the work gloves and threw them in the trailer. That's when George announced I was gonna have to walk back.

'Whaddya mean, walk?'

'Can't pull you *and* the trailer. I'll meet you back at the campground.'

'You ain't gonna do a number on me, are you, George?' I said.

'Hey, I was in the Air Force. We got a code of honor.'

'I thought you was in the Army.'

'I never said I was in the Army. The Army starts battles, the Air Force finishes 'em. You wanna see my tattoo?'

'Christ,' I said. 'Gimme the Old Grand-Dad. I ain't walkin' alone.'

He took a hefty swig and handed it over to me.

'And, if it's all the same to you, I'll hold on to this.'

I reached into the trailer and lifted his old hip out, holdin' the jar up to the moonlight. It was spade shaped, with a hole in one end where a femur once nestled, twisted like some child's mangled sand shovel. Bits of gristle still clung to it, as well as dried blood. There were at least a half dozen small fractures woven through it, which someone had marked with numbers and arrows. It looked like somethin' Leonardo da Vinci might have designed if he was a forensics expert.

'Oh man, I tell you what,' George said. 'That's fucking low. Take a man's hip for ransom.'

'If you ain't back at that campground,' I said, 'I'm gonna use it to drive golf balls.'

He climbed on the Gold Wing and crept off into the night. A hundred yards down the highway, he flipped on his lights and the whole fuckin' bike lit up like a moth magnet. I took a big pull of bourbon and stood there for a moment, listenin' to crickets. Then I hoisted George's hip-in-a-jar on my shoulder and started hoofin' it down the highway.

By the time I reached the turn-off toward Brushy, I was fairly well liquored up and my shoes were full of gravel. I

116

plopped down by a fence-post and stared up that black road toward the prison. 'So much for rehabilitation,' I thought to myself. 'Outta the can five hours and already back on the game.' I wondered if that was some kind of record for recidivism. I could just make out the lights of the guard tower and I sat down and leaned against a fence-post, chucklin' to myself 'cause I wasn't on the other side of that guard tower. All them crickets in the grass were laughin' right alongside me.

The fence I was leanin' against ran along the side yard of the women's shelter. I could see the White-Haired Gal's laundry still hangin' on the line. I stared up into the darkened windows of the house, wondrin' which room she was asleep in. Then, and I'll never know why for sure, I decided to write her a letter.

I pulled out my writin' paper and pen from my shirt pocket and sat there in the moonlight composin':

Hello, White-Haired Girl,
    It's the middle of the night, I'm leanin' against a fence-post and felt the urge to write you this letter. Earlier today, I saw you in the yard. I ain't seen a woman – any woman – for nine months and you appeared like a vision.
    Lord knows what someone's done to you to cause you to end up in this place. I can't imagine it being that much fun. Hell, you probably can't even have pillow fights with each other! It probably dredges up too many bad memories!
    I just hope you know that not all men are fuckin' animals. Me, for instance, I ain't never hit a gal. I don't know what drives a man to domestic violence. Some people— Wait, a light just came on! I wonder if it's yours. Okay, it's gone. Some say they get it from their

daddies. My daddy used to hit me with a medical dictionary, and sometimes a thesaurus. I think it rubbed off on me as you may have noticed my excellent vocabulary! My momma would step in and grab me up in her arms and say to my daddy, 'If you hit him, you better hit me first,' and I would think, 'Great, now he's got a choice of targets!' And sure enough, with my momma holdin' on to me, we'd both get thumped. Then my mom would run upstairs and cry. Women ain't always the best peacekeepers. It's true, men instigate violence, but they are also better at negotiating peace. Which is why the head of the UN is always a man and never a woman, 'cause you can't work out a treaty if you're upstairs hidin' under the bed. Maybe, I'm ramblin' on account of I'm a bit drunk. But I just think you should know,

I'd run out of paper! 'Oh man,' I thought, 'this isn't gonna make any sense if I can't finish it.' I looked over at the laundry on the line. It seemed like my only option. I flopped over the fence, pulled down a pair of white underwear, draped them across my knee and tried to wrap things up concisely.

to me, you're a beautiful gal. I reckon a lot of men would probably view you, a battered woman, as damaged goods, you know, kind of like a dented can of creamed corn at the grocery store. But hell, on the inside, I know you are still perfectly good creamed corn. That's pretty much all I had to say.

Otis Lee Creanshaw

PS Apologies for writin' on your unmentionables but I ran out of paper. I hope this washes out.

I clothespinned the note to the underwear and hung it back on the line. Then I started back down the road to the campground.

When I got there, George was asleep in the tent, snorin' like a tractor. He'd unhooked the trailer and draped the tent cover over it. I stretched out on the picnic table and passed out under the stars.

In the mornin', he shook me out of a bourbonitis fog.

'Where's my hip?' he was yelling. 'My hip? Where's my hip. Where's my hip?!'

'Let go a me,' I said.

I told him I wasn't sure but I think I'd left it by the fence outside the women's shelter. He didn't ask what I'd been doin' at a women's shelter in the middle of the night. He just wanted his goddamned hip back.

'We got to find it,' he said. He was a little panicky. I guess I couldn't blame him. If it was my hip, I'd be upset too – even if the thing was fairly useless.

We drove out to the shelter and searched all along the fenceline. George started kickin' at a fence-post, cursin' and wheezin'. Some kind of separation anxiety, I suppose.

'It ain't here!' he cried. He got down on his knees and started flailin' in the high grass along the highway. 'Somebody's done carried it off!' You'd have thought he'd lost the world's most precious archaeological find – the fuckin' Dead Sea Scrolls or somethin'.

'Don't worry, we'll find it,' I said, tryin' to calm him down. I saw that the clothesline was empty. I reckoned the White-Haired Gal had gotten my letter.

Suddenly, a barrel-necked rhinoceros of a woman came marchin' across the yard. I figured her for the caretaker or the Big Mama or whatever you called someone in charge of

119

battered women. She came right up to the fence-rail and eyeballed me fiercely.

'I'll betchoo better clear out 'fore I get the law over here,' she announced.

'No trouble, ma'am,' I said and, believe me, I didn't want any. 'We're just lookin' for somethin'.'

'Lookin' to get your scrawny ass shot,' the Big Mama said. 'I keep a twelve-gauge in the house. So I'm tellin' you nice the first time. Scram.'

'Lady . . .' I said, raisin' my hands, tryin' to be peaceful.

'Don't lady me. You the one creepin' round here in the middle of the night writin' self-confessionals on girls' underwear?'

I didn't really know what to say to that, and I guess she took that as a yes. Frankly, I was a little peeved. As far as I was concerned, that letter was private correspondence. Behind me, George popped out of the grass.

'Otis!' he yelled. 'Ask her if she's seen it!'

'Otis, is it?' The Big Mama said, clockin' me. By now, a cluster of battered gals had gathered outside to see what all the commotion was about. They'd heard George call me 'Otis' and now they were all agitated, chatterin' like a box of turkeys. I bet they'd *all* read my letter.

The Big Mama said, 'I'm within my rights to put a load of buckshot in your ass you cross this fence again. That goes for the both of you twisted perverts.'

'We ain't perverts,' I said to her.

Then George called out, ''Scuse me, ma'am, you find a human hip around here anywhere?'

'That's it,' she said. She turned to the girls and shouted, 'Somebody go inside, get the twelve-gauge.'

But they didn't move. Instead, one of the girls called up in the direction of an upstairs window.

'Brenda, honey! Your United Nations Ambassador is down here!'

Ah, I thought, another Brenda. Then I saw her, framed in the window, eyes like polished slate. Amid all the hubbub she seemed perfectly imperious. She was standin' there with her hands on her hips, watchin' the whole thing. I couldn't help myself, I smiled at her and waved. She vanished from the window.

The Big Mama saw that gesture and her neck throbbed with pure rage. I figured maybe it was best we hightailed it. George came huffin' over to the fence. He'd been too preoccupied with locatin' his missin' body part to take in what was going on. He surveyed all the gals in the yard and said, 'What is this, a whorehouse?'

The Big Mama had definitely had enough. She wheeled and headed briskly for the house, and I knew from experience it was the walk of someone goin' for their shotgun. She tried to herd the girls back inside but they just lingered in the yard.

'Any you whores seen my hip?' George called out.

'Let's go,' I said. 'Your hip ain't here.'

We headed back to the bike. George looked like he wanted to cry. We climbed on, George turned the engine over and, fuck me, that bike must've had some nasty tailpipes, because it started as loud as a shotgun. Something pinged off my football helmet and I looked back at the house to see Brenda in the window, smoke curlin' out of the twelve-gauge double barrel tucked against her shoulder.

That night, we hauled the trailer full of copper up into the woods of Frozen Head State Park, a half mile or so above the campground, to burn off the insulation. The flames gave off every color imaginable, a real chemical extravaganza. George swayed disconsolately over the fire. He'd been depressed all day, and I'd apologized about a thousand fuckin' times for losin' his hip, but he couldn't seem to get over it.

'George, I know how you feel,' I said. 'I once had me a baseball signed by Willie Mays. When I lost it, I never forgave myself.'

Actually I'd pawned it.

'But, hell, it ain't like you're ever gonna be able to use that old smashed hip again or nothin'.'

George looked at me hard.

'Well, I'll tell you what,' he said.

'What?'

He lowered himself awkwardly on to a sofa-sized rock, where someone had spray-painted in vivid orange: 'VIRGIL IS AN ASHOLE'. Below that, smaller scribblings, in varyin' handwriting, backed the opinion.

'That hip, that you've so casually dismissed as a trinket . . .' George said, 'happened to be my annuity.'

'How so?'

'How so? I'll tell you how so.' Then he poured out his hard-luck story. 'Ever since I was a kid, I wanted to be a jet pilot. My daddy used to say to me "Kid, in the Army, you get pie every night. All the pie you can eat." But I didn't wanna eat pie. I wanted to fly F-14 Tomcats, B-52 Stratofortresses, C-119 Flying Boxcars. I could tell you the wingspan and payload of any plane flyin' overhead. I'd look up at them carving up that sky and think to myself, "That's how I wanna see the world, looking down on it."

'So, come eighteen, I go in to the recruiting station – this was in Dayton, Ohio – and told 'em I wanted to go to Nam. They said "yessiree" and I tell you what, they knew I was never gonna see the inside of a cockpit. They lied like a bad toupee.

'I did basic training at Lackland, Texas, and, approximately fifty thousand sit-ups later, took the honors graduate test. They said my verbal skills were outstanding, top of the mark. I asked when do I go to flight school? They said, you're not going to flight school, you're going to Eglin AFB in Las Vegas – the middle of the friggin' desert – to learn Human Relations. I said what's "Human Relations"? They said "recruitment". I said I didn't want to be a recruiter, I wanted to be a pilot. They said well that's tough titties.

'So I ended up at Recruitment School where they taught me how to convince youngsters if they joined the Air Force they could fly.'

'Salesman, eh?' I said.

'In a manner of speaking, that would be correct,' George replied. 'I finish Recruitment, where do you think they post me?'

'Where?'

'Two miles down the road, at the Armed Forces Recruitment Center, smack dab in the middle of the Las Vegas Strip, right between the casinos. I showed up for duty and the Chief Recruitment Officer said, "Lively, every ignat who's just blown his wad at the roulette table is gonna come in here and try to join up 'cause he's broke and desperate. Your job is to talk 'em out of it. Send 'em over to the Army desk, send 'em to the Navy desk, send 'em back to Nebraska, just don't let 'em into the Air Force." '

'That's crazy,' I said. 'Gamblers. Risk takers. *Exactly* what the Air Force needs.'

'You'd be right. But no, I had to *anti-recruit* them. I probably turned away enough recruits to win the Vietnam War.'

George took a swig of bourbon, then rose and hobbled over to the fire to stir the copper around with a tree branch. It was pliant now, like spaghetti. He pushed it into a lump. It gleamed like a hill of new pennies.

'I was quartered at the Sahara Casino. That's where the Air Force put me up. The rooms were cheaper than military housing. But because I was on duty, I wasn't allowed to walk through the casino. They made me use the employees' entrance. So I'm living in a casino hotel, but I'm not allowed to be *in* the casino. Every day for two years, I'd come out, cross the street and go to work in the middle of the strip. That was the full extent of my Air Force experience. The day my discharge was supposed to come through, I said to myself, "Fuck it," and cut through the casino on the way to work. An armed guard came around the corner, wheeling a metal money cart, and smacked right into my hip. Shattered it in half a dozen places.'

George took another swig of bourbon and stared into the fire. The heat had curled the dead bugs on his jacket into crispy insignias. He began haphazardly pickin' them off and chuckin' them into the fire.

'The VA gave me a new plastic hip, that was the extent of it. I went to see a legal advocate. He said the Air Force wasn't gonna give me any compensation, other than retirement pension. One hundred and fifty-six dollars a month. Said I had no business in the casino as I was on active duty. And the Sahara wouldn't pay out because I wasn't supposed to be there. As far as they was concerned, it was an Air Force matter, which left me, effectively, with my tail in the crack.'

George turned away from the fire and limped over toward me, extending the bourbon. His story seemed to have exhausted him.

'I've spent the last five years goin' back and forth with the Sahara, the VA, the Air Force . . . the whole shooting match, and won't one of them throw me a goddamned bone, you'll pardon the expression. I bought me this Gold Wing three years ago and I been livin' on one hundred and fifty-six dollars a month and whatever I scrape together through pure self-initiative, and I'm fed up with it.'

He motioned for the bottle back. 'So, for a year now, I've had this plan. I'm going back to Vegas, and I'm gonna set up a protest display out in front of the casino – picture this.' He was reinvigorated now, conjuring excitedly with his hands, 'There'll be a card table. Some sketches, tastefully displayed, of me undergoing hip surgery. And one framed one of me in my Air Force uniform, dress blues. The center-piece *was going* to be my shattered hip, surrounded by minia-ture flags, a blending of wounded patriotic pride and human wreckage. The casino ain't gonna like me scaring off customers. I reckon they'll settle sooner than later.'

'Sounds like a good plan,' I said.

'That hip,' George said, despondently, 'was going to be the showstopper. Without that, I'm just gonna look like some ranting lunatic.'

I didn't know what to say now. I felt shittier than ever.

Next mornin', George hauled the clean copper down to Knoxville to scrap it. He wouldn't be back until the after-noon, so I waited around by the campground until I got restless and decided to walk into town.

I was thinkin' about the huge pile still sittin' there at the REA. I was thinkin' if we had a truck, we could haul it all off, a one-shot deal.

When I got to the Ford dealership in town, I scanned the lot. There were a couple of new F-350s sittin' there, and that was a truck I knew inside out. They'd never notice if we took it for a midnight test drive.

*   *   *

Brenda the White-Haired Gal was in the coffee shop. I saw her through the window, sittin' at a table with a couple other gals. And don't you know, I went right inside and up to her and said it seemed to me like we'd gotten off on the wrong foot. The three of them bristled. I could feel the manhate steamin' off that table but I wanted her to know I didn't have no hard feelings about her shootin' at me. Then I turned around and left and walked over to the bus station just to check the schedule and while I was standin' there, she came in on her own.

'You're messin' with a load of hornets,' she said.

'I hear you,' I said.

'I hope you do. 'Cause you got no inkling of how nasty them girls are.'

'Where'd you learn to handle a shotgun? I know you coulda shot me you wanted to.'

'Anyone else there would've. It was just rock salt. Round here that's what's known as a handshake.'

'Well, thanks,' I said. 'Apologies for scribblin' all over your underwear. I got a little carried away with inspiration.'

'They weren't mine,' she said. 'How *big* does my ass look?'

Her jeans were about a size too small. She didn't want someone to notice that, she'd have bought the proper size. So she wasn't a complete manhater.

'Coupla short sentences,' I said. 'Really tiny writing.'

'They was my roommate's, Roberta's,' she said. 'You could write a novel on her panties.' Then she laughed; her first amiable gesture. If you ever want to break the ice with a gal, get her to talk about another gal's ass – works every time. Women the world over are constantly judgin' each other's asses. That's probably where the word *assess* comes from.

'I'd stay away from that house, I was you,' she said, and walked out.

I watched those size-too-small jeans leavin'.

'Maybe, I see you again, I'll just say hello!' I called out.

George got back that afternoon. He handed me two one-hundred-dollar bills and some loose singles, reluctantly, like someone foldin' on a good poker hand. I reckoned he'd spent the drive to Knoxville reevaluating his financial prospects.

We sat there at the picnic table and drank some bourbon. *Johnny Cash: Live at Folsom Prison* was playin' from the bike. There were some kids splashin' around in a wadin' pool next to a set of swings. These campgrounds catered mainly to families. All the sites were filled with Winnebagos and Airstreams, and George's saggy tent looked like a party-crasher.

'You got family, George?' I said.

'Spread around here and there.'

'Wife?'

'Traded her for the Gold Wing.'

'Kids?'

'That'd be the trailer.'

'Any place seem like home?'

'Not generally, no,' said George. 'Home don't really mean all that much unless you're backpedaling. I'm seeing this country laid out in front of me. When I'm done with that, there's others. Why you asking?'

'I don't know. Seems it might be nice to settle somewhere.'

'You talking about yourself now?'

'We could clear out that whole stash of copper. That's a good chunk of cash.'

'I've been thinkin' the same thing myself,' said George.

'We'd need a truck.'

'That we would.'

'I can get us a truck. The Ford place here in town.'

'Steal?'

'Borrow. Today's Friday. They're closed tomorrow. We burn the copper tonight, take it down to Knoxville tomorrow mornin', have the truck back on the lot by tomorrow night.'

'What if the scrappers is closed tomorrow?'

'Haul it in Monday. Then, I reckon, ditch the truck in Knoxville.'

He thought about it.

'We'd be veering toward what is commonly referred to as an Industrial Felony,' George said, almost to himself. 'Up to now, I've been able to assuage my petty criminal activities.'

'Even Johnny Cash was a felon,' I said.

The clearing where we burned the copper was littered with beer cans from teenage forays, plus a smattering of bottles featuring the brands of choice for tramps on a budget: Old Crow, Rebel Yell, Early Times, MD 40-40, Night Train. It was surrounded by somber old hickories, whose leaves, at the moment, were wiltin' in the heat of the massive bonfire George and me had made.

Chopper McFadgeon, my old buddy, would have called what we did half-assed. I'd bought a hacksaw blade and wire-cutters from the True Value, and cut a notch in the blade to make a jimmy. Turns out the trucks on the lot weren't even locked. I picked out a feisty red F-350, hotwired it, and then hit a snag. All the vehicles had some kind of sales chatter written on the windshields. The red one, for instance, said 'ALL THE BELLS AND WHISTLES!!'. I tried scrapin' it with the jimmy but it must've been special paint. Finally, I just eased the truck off the lot, turned in to an Amoco Station and tried to clean it off with soap and water.

A lanky-looking attendant, with pork-chop sideburns like Tom Petty, came out and watched me for a while. He never said a thing, just leaned against the pump with a look of permanent surprise. Finally, I gave up, bought ten dollars' worth of leaded, and drove out to the campground to pick up George. He saw 'ALL THE BELLS AND WHISTLES!!' on the windshield and just stood there, stunned, with his palms turned out like he was checkin' for raindrops or somethin'.

'It don't come off,' I said. 'Let's just get this done!'

We drove through town, prayin' we didn't pass no cops. When we got to the REA, I cut through the fence with the wire-cutters and we cleaned it out in under an hour.

Rather than throw the coils on gradually, George had elected to burn three-quarters of a ton of copper at once. He'd drenched it in gasoline, thrown a match, and the thing went up like a napalmed hut. The intensity had backed us both up against a tree and now it was threatenin' to set the entire Frozen Head State Park ablaze.

When he started attackin' the fire, I realized he was drunk. He was into his second bottle of Old Grand-Dad. He wielded it in one hand and, with the other, flayed at the flames with a tree branch, desperately tryin' to condense it into a manageable conflagration. He'd stripped down to boxers and cowboy boots, sweat streamin' off him like glycerin. His furious shadow against the canopy of tree leaves was cinema-sized, like somethin' dreamed up for World Wrestling.

'You ought to get back from that fire a ways,' I warned. Flames were dancin' around his feet. I'd retreated to the truck about twenty yards away, still tryin' to figure out how to get the writin' off the windshield. Gasoline hadn't worked. We weren't goin' to get far down the Knoxville

Highway with 'ALL THE BELLS AND WHISTLES!!' splashed across the truck.

George started singin' 'Ring of Fire', still flailin'. He seemed resigned to the idea we were fucked.

'We're as good as sitting ducks,' he sang, fittin' it in nicely before, 'Oh, but the fire went wild'. He seemed, momentarily, to have lost interest in the real fire, the one he was practically standin' in. He crooked the bourbon bottle to his lips and sweet-talked it.

'Hello, my amber beauty. Give Daddy a big kiss. Daddy loves you very much.' He took a staggeringly long drink, then wiped his mouth with the back of his hand. 'This ain't how I envisioned my life panning out,' he mumbled.

'George, bring the bourbon over here,' I called.

'Fuck off,' he said, and cradled it to his armpit.

'The alcohol might work as a solvent.'

'And if it don't, we're out good bourbon. On top of everything else.'

He wasn't actin' right. I went over to get the bourbon from him. He swung at me with the branch.

'Stay away from me,' he warned. 'You already took my hip.'

'I need the bourbon,' I said. 'Come on, get away from the fire.'

'Your arrival in my life has been an invasion,' he sang.

I took a step forward.

'And your presence now is abusive.'

He was leanin' at a weird angle, his cracked teeth formin' an agonizing O-shape, like some kind of tragedy mask. Slowly, he surrendered the bottle.

I went back to the truck and poured some of the Old Grand-Dad on to the paint, then wiped at it with my shirtsleeve. The lettering began to smear.

'It works!' I cried out.

'Good Lord,' I heard George mutter.

I took off my shirt and used it to clean. I'd managed to get most of 'WHISTLES!!' off the glass when I heard George give out a low exhausted wail. I looked over to see him lurchin' to one side, clutchin' his waist. His body was roughly the shape of a boomerang.

'I tell you what . . .' he said.

'What?' I yelled. He looked like he was about to puke his guts out. As disgustin' as that is, you're always compelled to watch. So I did. But he didn't vomit. It was something else. He looked up at me like I owed him some kind of explanation.

'I think my hip's done melted,' he announced.

We drove through the night to Knoxville with George propped unevenly against the truck door. He claimed his hip was now congealed somewhere near his bladder and, every twenty minutes or so, I had to pull over and help him out of the truck to take a leak. He didn't look like a man peeing. He looked like he was watchin' a train come around the bend.

We got to the scrappers, sat in the truck waitin' for it to open, then cashed in 1600 pounds of copper. It came out to about seventeen hundred dollars apiece. I reckon they knew it was stolen, and I reckon they didn't care. Then I drove back to Knoxville. George snored convulsively the whole way.

When we got to the campground, I told him I thought he oughta get to a hospital. But I already knew he wouldn't. I packed the tent and his belongings into the trailer, backed the bike up to it and helped him on.

The last thing he said was he thought he now presented an extremely convincing testimonial to Workplace Indifference and he would write from Las Vegas.

I reminded him I didn't have an address.

'You're better off that way,' he said, and drove off, leanin' precariously to the right. He looked like he was never goin' anywhere but in circles.

I got the truck back to the Ford dealer. Someone was goin' to have to explain 240 unaccounted odometer miles.

I felt breathless and vaguely dissatisfied. Troubled, I guess would be the right word. I thought about Brenda the White-Haired Gal, and what she'd said at the bus station after I'd said, 'Maybe, I see you again, I'll just say hello.'

What she'd said was, 'We'll see.'

Three Chords

Some people's names says everything you need to know about 'em: Smokey Robinson, Chubby Checker, Dusty Rhodes, Johnny Paycheck, Evel Knievel (poor bastard never learned to spell).

My daddy's name was Jack Daniels Crenshaw. My grandaddy's name was Johnson Johnson (J.J.) Crenshaw. Both of them made prominent names for themselves around Sevier County as reliable Saturday-night jailfillers, predictable as the calendar.

If you wanna be remembered in this life, use your *full* name. All *three* of them. A three-word name leaves a lyrical imprint. It has cadence: Lee Harvey Oswald, James Earl Ray, Mark David Chapman. There's a reason you remember those names – aside from the fact they were all world-class assassins. No one would remember the guy who shot JFK if he had just called himself Lee. The only one-named assassin anyone remembers is Brutus. (Sirhan Sirhan doesn't count. That was one name twice.) If he had gone by three names, Brutus Wayne Henson, for example, he'd probably stand out a lot more prominently, not just as some Shakespearean second banana.

It's up to the public to decide who deserves one-name status and there's only three people who have rightfully earned it: Elvis, Ali and Liberace.

No one changed music as much as Elvis. I ain't sayin' he was a genius and I ain't sayin' he was the King, 'cause he wasn't. If he's the King, how come he's buried in his own backyard like a hamster? But he was *King Creole* in 1964. And, in that movie, he starts singin' in the middle of a ninety-five dollar store robbery – probably the only time in cinema history that an impulsive musical number has spoiled a felony. In *Jailhouse Rock*, his singin' kicks off a prison riot. In *GI Blues*, it quells a bar-room brawl. And, in one of the most amazin' displays of lyrical acuity ever, *Blue Hawaii*, he whips open a music box and uses it to back himself on 'I Can't Help Falling in Love'. Try that on stage some night.

I watched those flicks as a kid. The plots had holes you could drive a car through, which was why they played at the drive-in. But I learned something valuable from Elvis: *an impromptu song has the power to change the course of an event.*

It was my own impromptu singin' that won Brenda the Devil Woman over. I'd aimed to leave town after the copper scam. But frankly, I didn't know where to go. Even though that pile of copper was missin' from the REA and sooner than later someone would start askin' around, I stayed – like a dog who's just peed on his territory. I had seventeen-hundred dollars and no plans to do anything but write songs. My only foreseeable project was unraveling the sweet misunderstandings of a woman. So I stayed in Wartburg.

I found a roomin' house at the edge of town called Mr G's, an old two-storied colonial house with a wraparound porch separatin' at the joists like it was tryin' to sail away. The owner, who I reckoned was Mr G – he never said – sat permanently behind his desk watchin' detective shows on a black-and-white TV. He seemed to be deeply drawn into each case's outcome. He would pull on his cigarette like it hurt his face.

'How much for a week?' I asked him, when I first walked in.

He didn't take his eyes off the cop show.

'It's a hunnert by the month. For that you can shit, go blind or piss up a rope.'

He led me upstairs to a room that smelled like old men. The ceiling had been dropped to around six feet, probably to discourage any serious consideration of hangin' yourself. The toilet was down the hall. I sat down on the saggin' mattress and tried to feel some sense of profound renewal.

I'd spotted an old upright piano in the lobby when I came in. But I couldn't imagine tryin' to plink on it with Mr G right there. So I went back outside, walked over to J. C. Penny's, bought myself a pair of Levi's and three cotton T-shirts, ate a plate of hash browns at the coffee shop and then headed back to Mr G's. When I got there, there was an old-timer sittin' on the porch pickin' an old Gibson.

He barely acknowledged me, just a slight flick of his head, a rhythmic impulse. I watched his yellowed fingers dance up and down the frets, and he stared back at me in a way that made me think I was makin' him sleepy. He was playin' an old hillbilly number, faintly recognizable, somethin' that reminds you of a car chase up a dirt road.

When he finished the song, I nodded to him to keep goin'.

'My home's across the Blue Ridge Mountains,' he said, in a reedy hogcaller voice. But it wasn't biographical information. It was the name of the tune he began pickin'. He only spoke to announce a song title, and it kind of added up to a protracted one-way conversation. 'Stay in Your Own Backyard'. 'Why Should I Cry Over You?'. 'My Daddy Was a Rabbit'. 'It Ain't No Lie'. 'Jenny Lind'. 'I Love You Best of All'. 'River, Stay Away From My Door'.

Hillbilly music comes from a place you'll never get back to. Rock and roll, blues, country and western – those are forms of fire. Hillbilly music is smoke. Ask yourself, what did people do before television, before record players, before radio? They played hillbilly music, that's what. Still, most of the world treats it as a joke, play-on music for a back-wash Dogpatch opera: the bumpkins in *The Beverly Hillbillies* or the randy mountain boys of *Deliverance*.

Deliverance was a peerless fuckin' great film. But all most people remember is the weird guy on the bridge with the banjo and Ned Beatty squealin' like a pig. What little progress the South has made in the last fifty years gets a kick in the teeth every time someone starts up 'Dueling Banjos'. So much for deliverance.

I asked him if he knew 'Turkey in the Straw'. He shook his head yes, but didn't play it. Instead he said 'I wish we'd never met' and I guess that was the name of that tune. I sat on the porch rail and watched him all afternoon.

The next day I went over to the pawn shop and bought a guitar, a derelict lookin' acoustic, no discernible make, covered in cowgirl decals. The woman who sold it to me made up a price on the spot, twenty dollars, and told me it would look good hangin' on a wall.

'I intend to learn how to play it,' I said. She looked at me the way you'd look at a grown man comin' down a playground slide. Like maybe he's a little long in the tooth for this activity.

'That thing's been in an' out of here more times than the flies,' she said. It sounded like a warnin' not to bring it back.

I took the guitar back to Mr G's. The old-timer was on the porch again, pickin' away. I waited for him to finish and asked him if he'd tune my guitar, which he did, wordlessly, and gave it back. Then I just held it in my hands like an idiot.

He started another tune and eventually I began plunking along atonally. The idea was to annoy him into helpin' me.

He stopped playin', reached over and curled my fingers into a G-shape. I banged on that for a while, then he showed me a C. Then a D.

By the end of the day I could hold my own to 'Arkansas Traveler' and 'Old Dan Tucker'.

Three chords. That's all you need for a serenade.

The songs I wrote for Brenda #3 make convenient bookmarks in a marriage doomed from the get go. It was doomed because I married an unhappy woman, and eventually made her unhappier. But damned if I didn't try my best.

A week after I bought that guitar, I saw her through the window of the coffee shop, sittin' with a coupla other gals from the He-Man Haters' Club. I hoofed back to Mr G's, grabbed my guitar then went back to the coffee shop.

Things, of course, didn't happen exactly the way they do in Elvis films. My first few chords didn't stop the action of all the diners. No one put down their forks and started snappin' their fingers. The cook didn't start drummin' on pots and pans and the waitress didn't materialize with a push-broom bass. In fact, everyone looked a little tense, Brenda most of all.

I just stood there and croaked a three-chord ballad at her. Some might even say it was a dirge:

> I'm an ordinary decent guy
> I stay up all night

I'm an ordinary decent guy
I never get in fights

If we walked down the street
And your eye was bruised
They'd know it wasn't me
I wouldn't be accused
I'm an ordinary decent guy

I'm an ordinary decent guy
I'm likable
I'm white trash
But I'm recyclable

I drink too much
And I should give up smokin'
But I know the Heimlich maneuver
If you were ever chokin'
I'm an ordinary decent guy
I think you should give me a try
You're an ordinary decent girl
We should give it a whirl
I'm an ordinary decent guy
[*improvised on the spot*]
And though your friends give me the evil eye
And prob'ly want me to die
I'm an ordinary decent guy

As I was singin', I was aware of some notable differences
between a real-life serenade and the sanitized Elvis versions.
For instance, Elvis's performances were never hindered by
friends of the person he was singin' to askin' him if he would
like a 'healthy kick in the nuts'. Also, no one tried to take
his order mid-performance.

*   *   *

Afterwards, I bolted out the door, mindful of a chilled silence in the coffee shop. I wasn't sure what I'd *expected* to happen. But I was pretty sure it wasn't gonna pay out no romantic dividends. The only two things I was aware of was a sickness in my gut and cold flopsweat invadin' my new T-shirt. I should take a bath, I thought. I should brush my teeth. I should shave my ugly face. I should practice a goddamned song over and over before dive-bombin' a strange gal with it. I should avoid, in the future, complicated situations of my own makin'. An impulse, I told myself, ain't a plan.

Brenda came out. I was still holdin' the guitar in the serenade position, like a sniper.

'Was that supposed to be funny?' she said.

'I think maybe it was unintentionally funny.'

'You must be on somethin'.'

'I ain't. How cool did that look?'

'You got a cigarette?'

I pried my fingers loose and fished around for my Marlboros. I lit one for her, one for myself and we both kind of stared at the pavement.

'I'm considering some sort of restraining order,' she said, ''cause you are crazy.'

'Would that be crazy in a menacin' way, or crazy in a Waylon and Willy kind of way?'

'I don't have my sense of humor today,' she warned.

'You ought to consider lettin' down your guard,' I said. Wrong choice of words.

'You don't know the first thing about what I oughta and oughtn't do.'

'How 'bout you come have a drink with me.'

'Why would I do that?' she said.

''Cause if you don't, I'm gonna start singin' again.'

We went up the street to a bar called the Mint. She took a seat near the window, the only lit part of the room.

'What'll it be?' I asked.

'I ain't drank in six months.'

'Bourbon, then. That's a reentry drink.'

'Okay. With Co-cola.'

There were a few silhouettes hunched over the bar. They were eyein' my guitar warily, like it might pose a threat to whatever joy was comin' out of the bottoms of their glasses. I ordered a bourbon neat and one with Coke and brought it back over. She was wearin' a yellow cottony dress, with palm fronds on it. In the light, I could see faint raised scars across her knees. I sat the guitar down beside me.

'What goes on in there?'

'Where?'

'That shelter.'

'Right now, we're being coached in how to gain the upper hand in a divorce, through prejudicial affidavits. Although that don't much apply to me.'

'What is it, a law school?'

'Law school, jail, detox mansion, dyke factory, you name it. First thing every mornin' before breakfast, we have to recite a poem. You oughta hear it.'

'Go on.'

She lifted her drink and downed almost half of it in one gulp. Then she recited a lament that would surely cast a pall over someone's bacon and eggs:

> I got flowers today. Last night he got drunk and
>   hit me.
> He said he was sorry and it wouldn't happen
>   again.
>
> I got flowers again today. Last night he got

drunk again and hit me. He promised he
would never do it again.

I got flowers today. Last night he killed me.

She downed the rest of her drink.

'Biggest load of horseshit I've ever seen,' she said, wavin'
her glass. 'I'll have another.'

I got her another drink.

'Live one, hunh?' the bartender said, intimatin' I was in
over my head. I took the drink back to her.

'Why don't you leave?' I said. Meanin' the shelter.

'Because it's the best place to be for the time being.'

'Can I ask you a personal question?'

'It ain't stopped you yet. You're gonna ask me who's been
hittin' me. Then you're gonna go all Clint Eastwood and tell
me what you'd do if you met up with him.'

'Actually, I was gonna ask about them scars on your knees.'

Self-consciously, she pulled the hem of her dress forward.

'Mediterranean Fever,' she said quietly.

'You're a Melungeon?'

'You know I'm a Melungeon.'

I wasn't sure until I saw the scars. Mediterranean Fever
was a Melungeon stigma. I reached out my fingertips and
ran them over the scars. It wasn't meant as a sexual gesture.
It was a way, maybe, of testing strange waters. She looked
at my fingers and swirled her drink.

'You think I'm in your hands now? You think mystery is
glamour?'

'I suppose I do.'

'What happens when I'm no longer mysterious?'

'I'm not much for lookin' ahead.'

'It would appear you're not.'

'Who's been hittin' you?' I said.

She took another drink.

'Maybe we ought to change the subject.'

'Alright. I'll sing you another of my compositions.'

'No you fuckin' will not.' She went all quiet.

'He's two years older than me,' she finally said. 'He's in the Morgan County lock-up right now. For sexual assault.'

'Oh.'

'He ain't exactly a boyfriend.'

'Umm.'

'You figurin' this out yet?'

'Oh, man.'

'He's my brother.' She downed her drink clumsily. Some of it went on to her dress.

'Get me another,' she said.

Deeper water, I thought. Deeper fuckin' water than I'd imagined. I reckon Elvis would have backed away from this particular storyline. She told me how she'd been livin' with her two brothers up on the Cumberland Ridge. One of them, Tony, had twenty acres of dope growin' up above the house. Alcohol, Tobacco and Firearms got wind of it and busted him. He got out on arraignment and came back home, convinced Brenda had snitched on him. He beat her up and raped her. Family Services put her in the shelter.

Now she was gettin' steadfastly hammered on Coke and bourbon, and I felt like I'd just opened up a floodgate.

Somehow, in my prudent scope of human evil, I hadn't pictured her beyond a victim of what you might call 'plain old' battery. Bruised, yes. Scarred, for sure, but still a gal whose bad fortune might be redeemed by an ordinary decent guy like me – as if my good intentions could eventually over-shadow whatever lousy hand someone else had dealt her.

But this was some seriously fucked-up shit. Because here, I was thinkin' to myself, was a poisoned woman. Beyond rescue. And there wasn't a goddamned thing I could do about it. And I felt like an asshole for thinkin' that. I felt like an asshole for being drawn to a gal just because of her exotic looks. *'Take time to know her, son.'* That's what my miniature Johnny Cash always said. Why, for once, can't I listen to that sonofabitch?

Usually when I feel like an asshole, I know, at least, it's of my own doing. This time I blamed society.

'So,' she said, 'I expect you'll be wanting to skedaddle now.'

'It wasn't your fault what happened,' was all I could think to say.

'Of course it weren't my fault!' she exploded. 'What, do you think I *let* him fuck me?'

'I only meant . . .'

''Cause we all know *that's what Melungeons do*! Yessiree, get out the corn likker, we're havin' us a Saturday-night *family* gettogether. Uncle Rapey 'n' Cousin Gropey 'n' Chesty 'n' Molesty 'n' Pokey 'n' Pawey . . . all of us fuckin' each other's brains out . . . !'

Her outburst now had the attention of everyone in the bar.

'Granpa! Get off your cousin an' come over here pay me some attention, ya selfish bastard!'

'We're right with you, sister!' someone yelled from a barstool.

''Cause we're too goddamn good lookin' to be wastin' this on outsiders.'

'Maybe you should slow down on them bourbon Cokes,' I suggested.

'An' maybe you should run as far fuckin' away from this shithole town as possible,' she said.

I took her advice.

Not because I'm a coward, but because, when I looked

out the window, I saw a half dozen Harriet Tubman hench-women crossin' the street toward the Mint. The Big Mama was leading the pack.

'Oh fuck,' I said.

Brenda looked out the window.

'Oh fuck is right,' she said.

She jumped to her feet and called to the bartender.

'There a back way outta here?'

'Past the shitters,' he said, pointin' toward a hallway.

'Watch yer mouth,' I cautioned him. 'There's a lady present.'

'Come on,' she said, grabbin' my arm.

I grabbed the guitar and we hustled down the hallway and out the back door. It wasn't clear who was rescuin' who.

Rocky Top

We took a Greyhound to Nashville. Got on the outbound dog and put those East Tennessee mountains behind us. The sky widened and the land began to fan out. I'd spent most of my life hemmed in by hills or stone walls and now I could see clear across the blushing green flatlands where rickety black barns advertised, 'See 7 States from Rock City' on their roofs.

We sat at the rear of the bus and stared out the back window, watchin' resentment on the faces of drivers caught behind us, furious at a vehicle keepin' the speed limit. At Sparta the bus driver stopped for snacks and new passengers. We stood in the parkin' lot and watched a man pull up in a pickup truck. There was a deer carcass in the bed. Its feet were stickin' straight out from rictus, like a four-poster bed. The man climbed out in huntin' camouflage, went into the bus station and reemerged a few minutes later in an evening tux. He climbed back in the truck and drove off.

At Woodbury a few passengers got off and we had the bus to ourselves, except for a gray-haired man at the front who kept talking to the driver even though the sign over the door said 'Do Not Talk to Operator While Bus is in Motion'.

I'd bought a fifth of Old Grand-Dad at a package shop across from the station in Sparta. By now it was dusk and the lightnin' bugs flickered along the roadside. Someone had once told me they always appear eleven minutes before official sunset. You can set your watch by that. We passed the bourbon back and forth and eventually Brenda was leanin' on me drunkenly for support, all the encouragement I needed to keel over until we were both writhin' around on the seat. In the back of my mind I was thinkin' I was the ideal man to bring out all the wrong things in this gal. Then it was dark – inside the bus and out – and it felt like a curtain comin' down on a couple of fucked up pasts, so we just went at it like jackrabbits while the old man up front droned on and on about his life.

'One good year . . .' he was sayin'. 'Is that too much to ask for? One goddamned good year?'

That was the last thing I remember hearin' before I passed out.

We moved into a motel in Nashville right behind a Kenny Rogers honey fried chicken franchise. Two weeks later, we went down to the County Registrar's office and got married. I wore a brand new Willie Nelson T-shirt and Brenda wore a pink dress. There was a batch of us, twelve newlyweds in all. A Justice of the Peace performed the ceremony, then leaned in my ear and said he gave it six months, tops. Then we walked outside, stood on the pavement and managed to get showered by some errant rice from another couple.

Six months my ass. It lasted twice that long.

Everything was titties and beer for the first few weeks.

Brenda seemed happy and I'd landed a huge showbiz deal.

It happened after my first nightclub performance, a try-out spot at Tootsie's Orchid Lounge. I sang 'Crawl Inside a Bottle' and a new song called 'Women Call It Stalking':

I'm only six foot one against this chart on the wall
But when she's identifyin' me I feel ten feet tall
There's five guys here but when she singles me out
It kinda' makes me feel special, makes me feel proud
Well she can put her finger on me
And the rest of her too
Any kind of attention from that woman will do

But women call it stalking
Women call it stalking
It's just selective walking
But women have a tendency to exaggerate
Gonna hug her, gonna mug her, gonna see her some
    more
Hey Judge read the charge just a little bit slower

She says she'll see me in court
I can't wait
She calls it a trial but I call it a date
When the judge throws the book
I'll pretend it's a bouquet
Hey, I'm gonna marry that woman some day
You can tell a woman that you love her face to face
Or you can do it with a phone call that can't be traced

Women like dinner, women like lunch
Women like roses that come in a bunch
Women like hedges and flowers and trees
But when you're standin' behind one they call the police

147

When I see her there'll be tears down my face
It might be love or it might be mace

But women call it stalking
Women call it stalking
Just the kind of attention
Gets you right back in prison
Gonna hug her, gonna mug her
Gonna see her some more
Hey Judge read the charge just a little bit slower

Afterwards, a fella with a massive beer gut came up to the bar where I was gettin' my free drink and handed me a card. He told me he needed someone to host a show the followin' night at Vanderbilt University.

'Can you play piano?' he asked.

I told him I played a little piano.

'Learn "Rocky Top" by tomorrow. I'll meet you at the gymnasium five p.m. sharp.'

He left and I looked at his card. It read 'Dwight Sparks Productions'.

I bought the sheet music to 'Rocky Top' at a shop down on Music City Row and learned it on a piano at a Baptist Church across from the motel. I stayed there all night practicing that damned song. 'Rocky Top' is the Tennessee State anthem. Play it, and Tennesseans will clap and sing along as automatically as a chicken dancin' on a hotplate.

Next afternoon, I walked over to the Vanderbilt gymnasium. It was empty, except for a herd of donkeys millin' about in the middle of the basketball court. Dwight Sparks bobbed among them. He wore a straw hat and a striped referee's shirt. He poured feed into buckets and cursed methodically at the donkeys.

'That's Flopsy, Mopsy, Dixie, Earlene, Lightnin', Oil Burner, Tempest, Clementine, Cleopatra and Scarlet,' he said. 'Learn them names and who's who. I don't expect you to get it right first time out but you got to know who's going to the basket.'

I didn't know what the hell he was talkin' about. He read it in my face.

'You never seen a donkey basketball game before?'

'Never,' I said, amazed. The donkeys were starin' off into space, probably wondrin' how they'd been swindled out of pastoral splendor for a lifetime of varnished arenas.

'Same rules as normal basketball,' Dwight pointed out. "Cept the players *got* to stay on the donkey all times. Your job is to call the game.'

'Who? What players?'

'I dunno. Some frat boys. They'll be here directly. It's a fund-raiser for so and so.'

He walked me over to the courtside where a Yamaha electric piano had been set up beside a small announcer's table.

'If a donkey stalls, play 'Rocky Top'. That gets 'em movin' every time.'

'How's that work?'

'It just does. It's how I've trained 'em. Go ahead, give it a try.'

I hovered over the keys and haltingly plunked the openin' run to 'Rocky Top'. The donkeys perked their ears and shuffled briskly. Half of them took off in the general direction of a basket. The other half kind of danced in place. I reckon they were more defensive players. Or maybe my 'Rocky Top' wasn't completely recognizable.

'The pay is fifty dollars per game,' Dwight said. 'If it works out, you're lookin' at upwards of two hundred games annually. I cover Middle and Eastern Tennessee, Northern Kentucky . . .'

I didn't mention that I wasn't allowed to go to Kentucky 'cause of my parole.

'Can I play some of my own songs?' I asked.

'No. They'd likely get distressed. Stick to "Rocky Top".'

So that was my first professional showbiz gig. Drunken frat dudes astride donkeys, tryin' to dunk a basketball. Dwight refereed the match, although his 'refereeing', for the most part, consisted of followin' the donkeys around and scoopin' up globular piles of fresh shit into a blue bucket. The crowd was convulsed. They thought it was the funniest damned thing they'd ever seen.

The final score was 12–6. Cleopatra pretty much dominated the offense.

Plows

Like I mentioned, Love at First Sight is a confidence trick of the heart. But Marriage at First Sight is a lot more rational than it sounds. After World War Two, thousands of men came home and married the first gal they met. They didn't care about courtship or datin' or 'takin' time to know her'. Gettin' your ass shot at tends to alleviate pickiness. (So does nine months in prison.)

Now, these soldiers that came home and married right away – they ended up with one of the lowest divorce rates in modern history. They made their choice quickly and stuck by it. They didn't put it off, thinkin', 'I'll just do this and this before I get married. I'll get a job, a car, a nice house, *then* I'll find me a wife.' Nope, Hitler had put things in perspective. In fact, Hitler's biggest mistake was puttin' off his own marriage 'cause he had this bug up his ass about crushin' Western Europe under his boot heel – *obviously* a stallin' tactic. Consequently, he had about three hours of matrimonial bliss before it was time to shoot himself in the head. That ain't exactly givin' marriage a chance!

Today, people get divorced 'cause they look around and

see all the other choices out there and think they can do better. That's what society has done. Given us too goddamn many choices. Choices of trucks, cable channels, trailer styles, snacks, titty bars, beers, bourbons . . . there's too much of everything and it makes you fuckin' fidgety. You always think you can do better. So you leave your woman, or she leaves you, and go off in search of somethin' better. It ain't your fault. It's society's.

When I got out of Brushy, I wasn't thinkin' about choices because in prison you don't get *choices*. There ain't no fuckin' menu in the mess hall. It's sheet cake or nothin'. You *know* what you're gettin'. That's conviction. That's why you're called a *convict*.

I threw myself into the marriage with conviction. My job was clear and blue pluperfect: keep Brenda happy. Now, how do you keep a melancholy woman happy? Simple: you purchase a book. Not *Men are from Mars, Women are from Venus* or *The Feminine Mystique* or any of that other insipid pseudo-psychological treewaste. Never buy a book if the author on the back cover has better teeth than you. If they're called 'self help' books, how come they were written by someone else? Nope, the best advice on treatin' women is in *Roget's Thesaurus.* Look up the word 'Love' and just follow the directions underneath:

> Care for, take pleasure in, take an interest in, value, prize, cherish, sympathize, revere, coddle, fondle, drool over, enjoy one's favors, dote, embrace, infatuate, appreciate, admire, think the world of, idolize, pamper, spoil, indulge, spoonfeed, smother [!], cosset, ogle, leer, lay siege to one's affections, etc.

That should keep you busy for a while. Handily, the results

of my actions can also be found in the thesaurus. Under the word 'Resentment':

> dissatisfaction, huffiness, ill humor, discontent, the hump, rancor, growing impatience, get one's monkey up, tiff, pique, acerbity, acrimony, virulence, irritation, irascibility, splenetic sullenness, pugnacity, snappish, grumbling, grousing, stroppy, gloomy, saturnine, choleric, irritable, fierce, fiery, hot-tempered, inflammable, quick-tempered, vinegary, scolding, waspish, brusque, abrupt, gruff, sour, dyspeptic, petulant, blue, down, down in the dumps, cantankerous, morose, grim, cloudy, sunless, misanthropic, lashing, stinging, taunting, quarrelsome, etc., etc., etc.

There are seventy-seven words for 'love' in the thesaurus and 459 for 'resentment'. What this means is that each 'love' action would result in 5.9 types of 'resentment'. For example, 'devotion' would get me:

1. rankling
2. discontent
3. snappishness
4. tetchiness
5. bellicosity
5.9 getting under one's ski—

There's an old sayin': The first marriage is for sex. The second is for children. The third is for companionship. The way I see it, all marriages should be your third marriage. Sex and children are by-products. They'll both turn out to be less than you expected and more than you hoped for. Or vice versa.

Companionship, on the other hand, is its own reward.

153

And your chances of gettin' along with someone are as blind as pickin' an onion at a grocery store. In fact, if you look closely at the word *companion*, you'll see the word *onion* in there. All onions look good at the grocery store. It's only after you start peelin' away at the layers that you'll know whether there's gonna be tears or not.

Brenda was as sweet as a new Vidalia onion. But peel those layers back and, man oh man, it was nothin' but bitterness and tears. I might as well have been a human squeegee. It ain't no big surprise that she was prone to melancholia. Christ, the gal had practically been born under a 'kick me' sign. But what I stupidly hadn't figured was how much it would affect me.

I just got dragged down. Once our little smokescreen of a honeymoon had faded, the black rain moved in like a permanent front.

It'd been a year and some change since I'd left prison. Now, I was in a new one: the Tennessee State of Depression. We'd found a furnished apartment over in Shadyside. I bought a used Ford Falcon, white and non-descript, but with a sturdy motor and a good radio. I was makin' an honest income from the donkey basketball circuit. By my own calculation, I'd performed 'Rocky Top' approximately four thousand times. I almost had it down perfectly. But Brenda kept going into black moods. I could always tell because she was fairly blunt about it. I'd say, 'You wanna beer, tastycakes?' and she'd say, 'I feel like I'm in a rudderless boat, sinking into the waves, with no land in sight. Just rough seas.' I ain't no psychiatrist but that didn't sound like Sugar Mountain.

When she got like that, she'd blame her period. It didn't seem like a period. It seemed like an ice age.

She'd mist laconically in the bedroom for days, or pad around not talkin' to me. She'd tell me to go out, get drunk, have a good time, but if I did, she'd rail at me when I got

154

back for abandonin' her. She was the Queen of the Dirty Look, the manipulative sulk. Her brother's trial was comin' up soon and she needed to go back to Morgan County. I worked out a deal with Dwight where I could meet up with him for the basketball gigs and we moved back to Wartburg, *to a goddamned trailer*. The Harriet Tubman gals started right in on her, workin' their He-Man Hater voodoo and tryin' to drive a wedge between us.

Now *I* was profoundly unhappy and that inspired a lot of songs. Unfortunately, they were all blues. I felt trapped in the Land of the Minor Chord.

I still believed in Marriage at First Sight. But I was thinkin' maybe it works better if the gal you marry is appreciative, not onerous – you know, like one of them Malaysian mail-order brides. Hell, if the two of you don't even speak each other's language, you've got a good coupla years of workin' through that before you can even start to peel away each other's layers.

A vicious caseworker named Althea Porter from Harriet Tubman's started comin' over to the trailer and sniffin' around for signs of spousal abuse. She was lookin' in the wrong one. Any neighboring trailer would have yielded better results, but she had it in for me. She accused me of forcin' Brenda to marry me under duress. She accused me of kidnappin' her from the shelter and taking her beyond jurisdictional boundaries, of jeopardizing the impending abuse case. She would show up wearin' a livid-red sweatshirt that read 'RAPE VICTIMS FOR JUSTICE!, drink coffee with Brenda at the kitchen table and eyeball my every move.

'You look like serial killer,' she said to me one mornin'.

'Bear in mind, that's my coffee you're drinkin',' I replied. 'You ought to be a bit more neighborly.'

'I ain't here as a neighbor. I'm here to see this girl through her ordeal.'

'Well, I guess we're on the same team, ain't we?' I said.

Brenda just sat there quiet, resolutely empty to what was goin' on. She didn't stand up for me, she didn't side with Althea. It was almost like she wasn't feelin' nothin' at all. All Althea wanted to talk about with Brenda was affidavits, litigation, appeal maneuvers. She didn't seem to have any interest in Brenda's state of mind or the fact that her family was bein' ripped apart. It was all just legal posturing. The Tubman Shelter got funding only if it kept a client base. So as much as it claimed to stand against women's abuse, it *needed* abused women to stay in business. My affectionate nickname for Althea, when she showed up at the doorstep, was 'The Mercenary'.

Althea convinced Brenda to see a county-appointed shrink. They met up a few times and then Brenda told me that the shrink wanted to see both of us.

When we got to the City–County complex, the shrink came out and introduced herself. She took Brenda into her office and told me to wait in the lobby. I leafed through a brochure on adopting racin' greyhounds and one on how to prepare your home and auto for cicada infestation. Every seventeen years, hordes of cicadas descend on East Tennessee. The noise alone, the brochure explained, could drown out the sound of a single-engine plane. They possessed notoriously weak eyesight and could fly into your face with the velocity of a golf ball.

'You may not like some of the things your wife has to say about you,' the psychiatrist warned. 'Brenda's told me you two don't spend much time together.'

'I'm in show business,' I explained.

'What do you feel like when he's away?' she asked Brenda.

'Like I want to sleep. To go to bed till he gets home.'

'Then you're happier?'

'I suppose. But I'm afraid of him.' She looked at me when she said that, then lowered her eyes to a spot on the floor.

'I agree to almost anything he says, to keep the peace.'

That was news to me. Peace?

'I feel like I'm switchin' back and forth all the time,' Brenda confessed. 'I need his approval and I hate myself for that. I think I'm getting an ulcer.'

'Where?' the shrink asked.

'In my stomach. Like stalagmites hanging down from my gut.'

'Those are stalactites, baby,' I said. 'Stalactites, down. Stalagmites up.'

'I would say you have an angry dependence,' the shrink said.

I couldn't believe she was sayin' this shit in front of me.

'I want you both to work on breaking this dependency,' the shrink said. Then she handed Brenda her car keys and told her to keep talkin' until she asked for them back. I wasn't allowed to interrupt. Then the shrink handed me the car keys and told me to talk for a while. All I could think, holdin' them keys in my hand, was how nice it would be to own a truck again. I wasn't much of a candidate for therapy.

Brenda kept seein' the shrink. Me, I stayed at home and read Margaret Mead, the anthropologist and author of *Sex and Temperament in Three Primitive Societies* and, I believe, *Gone With the Wind*. If we were gonna rely on third-party advice in our marriage, I was gonna go with someone with published credentials, not some county-appointed matron with a brand new Volvo. Margaret Mead was married three times. I *believe* that makes her somewhat of an expert. Also, she had bad teeth.

Long before *Men are from Mars, Women are from Venus*, Margaret wrote a book called, simply, *Men and Women*. It was about *earthlings*. And it explained how the plow changed everything. A long time ago, women tended the crops with simple implements. Because they did the cultivating, they held the power. Then someone came along and invented the plow, which required more strength. The plow was hooked up to an ox or a horse and soon there was a grain surplus, which allowed women to tend the household and men to figure out what to do with the excess grain, which led to the invention of beer, whiskey and bourbon. So when men took over the farmin', the power shifted. It's been that way ever since. And that explains everything you need to know about a woman's feelings of dependency and inadequacy. Women ain't Venusians and Men ain't Martians. If anything, Men are Plows and Women are Hoes. But I'd keep that to myself if I was you.

My point is, Man ain't stronger than Woman. But a man plus an ox or a horse is.

IN THE CHANCERY COURT OF MORGAN COUNTY, TENNESSEE, AT WARTBURG

Otis Lee Crenshaw vs. Brenda Crenshaw

Judge: Hon. Roslyn Turnblatt
Plaintiff: Brenda Crenshaw
For the Plaintiff: Althea Porter, advisor
For the Defendant: Otis Lee Crenshaw, representing himself

OFFICIAL HEARING TRANSCRIPT

JUDGE TURNBLATT: Good morning, Althea.

ALTHEA PORTER: Morning, Rosie. Your Honor.

JUDGE TURNBLATT: How's the kids?

ALTHEA PORTER: Billy lost another tooth. He's down to seven, now.

JUDGE TURNBLATT: Snaggletoothed, hunh?

ALTHEA PORTER: Mouth like a hillbilly graveyard.

OTIS LEE CRENSHAW: 'Scuse me, Your Honoress.

JUDGE TURNBLATT: Yes?

OTIS LEE CRENSHAW: Is this a court or a dentist waiting room?

159

JUDGE TURNBLATT: I assumed we were waiting for your representative to show up.

OTIS LEE CRENSHAW: I'm representing myself.

JUDGE TURNBLATT: I see. Alright, I have this temporary restraining order served by the Clerk of Court on February 14th. Where was this served?

OTIS LEE CRENSHAW: Outside the White Hen Pantry. The clerk drove in when I was filling up. Handed it to me from his car window.

JUDGE TURNBLATT: And you then used it to clean your windshield?

OTIS LEE CRENSHAW: Well the pumps didn't have no towels.

JUDGE TURNBLATT: You realize this is an extremely serious document.

OTIS LEE CRENSHAW: I do. But seeing as how it came from a third party and not directly from my wife, I was a bit POed at the time.

JUDGE TURNBLATT: The Harriet Tubman Women's Shelter believes you represent a direct threat to your wife. It's somewhat rare for a third party to initiate an RO, and I'm inclined to dismiss this on the grounds that they do not have a strong enough position to pursue a case. But I want to make sure first. I want to ask your wife a few questions. Mrs Crenshaw?

BRENDA CRENSHAW: Yes, Your Honor.

JUDGE TURNBLATT: How are you?

BRENDA CRENSHAW: Fine, Your Honor.

160

JUDGE TURNBLATT: No, I mean how *are* you?

BRENDA CRENSHAW: Frankly, I'd like to go back home, Your Honor.

JUDGE TURNBLATT: But you agreed to this restraining order.

BRENDA CRENSHAW: I did at the time. I thought a night in jail might teach him a lesson.

JUDGE TURNBLATT: What happened the night your husband was arrested?

OTIS LEE CRENSHAW: Can I answer that, Your Honor?

JUDGE TURNBLATT: No you can't. Keep still.

BRENDA CRENSHAW: Well, he'd been drinking a little.

JUDGE TURNBLATT: How much?

BRENDA CRENSHAW: I'd say half a bottle of Old Grand-Dad.

JUDGE TURNBLATT: And?

BRENDA CRENSHAW: That's it. He was drinking. He does stupid things when he's drinking.

JUDGE TURNBLATT: Such as?

BRENDA CRENSHAW: Well, I was in the kitchen so I didn't exactly see what happened. But apparently he was trying to call someone in India.

JUDGE TURNBLATT: India?

BRENDA CRENSHAW: One of them sex lines.

OTIS LEE CRENSHAW: It wasn't a sex line!

BRENDA CRENSHAW: Yes, it was. 'Hindu Honeys'.

161

OTIS LEE CRENSHAW: It was a mail-order bride company! They ship you a wife for five hundred dollars. I was doing research on mail-order brides. For a song I'm working on. That's all.

JUDGE TURNBLATT: I'm talking to your wife, Mr Crenshaw. The one beside you. Not the one who comes in a crate. Mrs Crenshaw, continue please.

BRENDA CRENSHAW: Anyway, he was trying to dial India and the country code is 91. But somehow he ended up dialing 911. And the police answered. It was a mistake, but he had one of them daytime yelling shows on the TV. Turned up real loud. Someone was screaming, 'He hit me, he beat me, he knocked me down . . .' and the police must've figured it was me.

JUDGE TURNBLATT: Then what happened?

BRENDA CRENSHAW: They showed up, and knocked on the door and he got all lippy with them.

OTIS LEE CRENSHAW: Can't a man drink in his own house?

BRENDA CRENSHAW: They come inside and asked if I was alright, did he abuse me, that kind of stuff. And he hadn't, but when I seen what he was up to - calling those Hindu girls - I didn't stand in their way when they elected to take him to jail. Like I said, I thought he might learn a lesson.

JUDGE TURNBLATT: How did this RO come about?

BRENDA CRENSHAW: Well, Althea here came over to the house - said she'd heard the 911 call on the police scanner. She wanted me to come back to the Tubman Shelter. I said everything was OK. She went away but then she come back later with this other woman from

162

Family Services and they tried to convince me that Otis had a drinking problem and I needed to get away from him and I should file for a restraining order and, like I said, I was mad and so I agreed to it.

JUDGE TURNBLATT: And now you've changed your mind.

BRENDA CRENSHAW: Yes.

ALTHEA PORTER: Rosie, Your Honor. Can I say something on Brenda's behalf?

JUDGE TURNBLATT: If Mrs Crenshaw agrees. Mrs Crenshaw?

BRENDA CRENSHAW: OK.

ALTHEA PORTER: I believe that Brenda is under a lot of duress and should not, under any circumstances, be allowed near her husband.

OTIS LEE CRENSHAW: This woman has been brainwashing my wife ever since I met her!

JUDGE TURNBLATT: I'm not talking to you, Mr Crenshaw.

ALTHEA PORTER: You're aware that Brenda here has a long history of abuse, both from her family and previous live-in boyfriends? Mr Crenshaw is repeating these same patterns. Mentally abusing her.

OTIS LEE CRENSHAW: Oh, for crying out loud.

ALTHEA PORTER: She's been suffering from depression ever since she married him. And he's been using that to his advantage.

JUDGE TURNBLATT: In what way?

ALTHEA PORTER: For monetary gain. He embarrasses her in public. He sings horrible songs about her.

163

OTIS LEE CRENSHAW: They're not horrible!

JUDGE TURNBLATT: Songs?

ALTHEA PORTER: He ridicules her.

OTIS LEE CRENSHAW: I don't ridicule her. I happen to have written fifteen songs about my wife. They ain't ridiculous.

ALTHEA PORTER: Violent, threatening songs.

JUDGE TURNBLATT: Both of you . . .

OTIS LEE CRENSHAW: What part is violent?

ALTHEA PORTER: The one about punching her until she's blue as a smurf!

OTIS LEE CRENSHAW: That ain't what it's about at all!

JUDGE TURNBLATT: Order! Both of you are to address me and not each other. Understood? Mr Crenshaw, what's the nature of this song?

OTIS LEE CRENSHAW: Well, it goes something like this . . . one, two, three, four, one two three . . .

JUDGE TURNBLATT: What are you doing?

OTIS LEE CRENSHAW: I'm getting the rhythm. Imagine a blues riff.

> Baby you're blue
> Baby you're blue
> Baby you're blue, blue, blue, blue, blue,
> blue, blue, blue, blue, blue!
> Did I mention you were blue?
> People stop, people stare
> People say Oh my good lookee there
> There goes the bluest gal on earth

Bluer than if George Foreman punched a smurf
You're the bluest of all women
So blue when you go swimming
You leave a residue
In the pool, baby you're blue.

JUDGE TURNBLATT: If it were in my power, I'd issue a restraining order against you ever singing. Has it occurred to you that depression is a very private matter and your making a public spectacle of your wife's condition is not a supportive gesture?

OTIS LEE CRENSHAW: You got to understand, Your Honoress, when I first met her she'd come out of Harriet Tubman's. She was, if you'll pardon me, black and blue. Now she's just blue. Which is an improvement. I've never treated her with nothing but gentle loving kindness. But when she gets down, it affects me and I end up writing these blues songs. It ain't my fault if they're not chirpy.

JUDGE TURNBLATT: Mrs Crenshaw, have you sought support counseling?

BRENDA CRENSHAW: Yes, I have. Family Services got me counseling.

JUDGE TURNBLATT: Has Mr Crenshaw accompanied you to any of these sessions?

BRENDA CRENSHAW: Well, he would drive me there. Then wait in the car.

JUDGE TURNBLATT: So he hasn't partaken in counseling?

OTIS LEE CRENSHAW: I've sought out professional advice on dealing with clinical depression.

JUDGE TURNBLATT: What advice?

OTIS LEE CRENSHAW: Knowing full well that she's prone to mood swings and emotional theatrics, I've let her assert her independence, but at the same time reassured her she has a home to come to. I never raise my voice. I carry her up and down the stairs because they frighten her. I've done my best to win her trust.

JUDGE TURNBLATT: Carry her up the stairs? Who told you to do that?

OTIS LEE CRENSHAW: The book I read. On depression.

BRENDA CRENSHAW: It wasn't a book about depression. It was called *Care and Adoption of Racing Greyhounds*.

OTIS LEE CRENSHAW: It was still good advice!

JUDGE TURNBLATT: I am going to throw this RO out. But, Mr Crenshaw, I suggest you curb your drinking, attend supportive counseling with your wife and stop writing these ridiculous songs. And Mrs Crenshaw, I want to stress that a restraining order is a very serious thing and not a form of vindication. Do you understand that?

BRENDA CRENSHAW: Yes, Your Honor.

JUDGE TURNBLATT: Both of you go home.

Thermals

The shrink eventually told Brenda she was sufferin' from anhedonia and put her on tryciclics. A word somewhere after 'tricycle' in the dictionary. Ever see a kid on a tricycle? He's in his own world, havin' the time of his life. That's exactly what tryciclics do to you. Keep you goin' round in tight, endless circles, until someone calls you in for lunch.

The shrink said it was doin' wonders for her. But she wasn't the same Brenda I'd married. Now she hummed quietly under her breath all the time and would serve a plate of ice cubes for dinner.

I took over in the kitchen. She would sit at the table, smilin' beatifically, just like those paratroopers in Brushy, ridin' the thermals.

'Eat your sandwich, baby,' I would say.

'My mouth is too dry,' she would reply, then make a face mask from the sliced bread.

Cicadas

In June of that year, I went down to Knoxville to see my parole officer. He shook my hand with insincere enthusiasm and told me the Tennessee Department of Corrections had rescinded my parole early. Then he handed me a letter that had come to him by way of Brushy.

'I'd see to that, if I was you,' he said.

I opened the envelope, and a postcard of a motel fell into my lap. There was a blue kidney-shaped pool in the foreground lookin' artificially lit. On the back of the postcard, it said Simpson's Motel, Atlantic City, New Jersey. Color TV. Air Conditioned. Coffee Shop.

Underneath, I recognized my Old Man's handwriting. It had a kind of ransom-note immediacy to it:

> Otis Lee:
> Dying of cirrhosis. You got any money you can get your hands on?
>
> J.D.

I went outside and stood on the immense stone steps of the courthouse annex and lit a cigarette. How the fuck did my Old Man know I'd been in jail? I hadn't heard a lick from him in ten years. All around me, government types, empowered by the sheer expanse of so much granite, lingered on the steps, chatting homespun legalese.

'Wellfur Services is traitin' that whole chislin' family like they was Dutch Uncles!' a loud man behind me exclaimed, in a drawl so stretched you couldn't tell if he was angry about Welfare Services or pleased.

'I huuurd that,' someone replied. The tonal path of East Tennessee speech begins high, makes a long downward arc, then ends flat: words coming down a slidin' board.

All these people, I thought, with a uniform intent. To make sure guys like me walk the line. And my daddy before that. And my grandaddy before that. Hell, I reckoned they'd both been up and down these steps a few times.

I drove back up to Wartburg, trying to think of one goddamned good reason to go see him, one decent thing the sonofabitch had ever done for me.

I thought about the time, in a fit of drunken goodwill, he had announced he was takin' me to Gatlinburg to get a proper steak. I was probably eight or nine. We drove through the mountains in his rusty Bonneville, a cavernous four-door capable of accommodating his pompadour. The radio was playin' country Christmas songs. It was late December and the roads were iced. I was starin' with bug-eyed wonder at all the lit-up houses along the highway, each one tryin' to outdo the next for sheer wattage. The Old Man sipped from a paper bag every chance a stretch of straightaway gave him a free hand from the steerin' wheel.

We kept passing billboards for the Steakhouse.

HURRY TO THE GREAT SMOKEY STEAK HOUSE!!
HOME OF THE 72-OUNCE RIB-EYE.

170

The sign featured a Flintstonian-sized steak lappin' over the edges of a platter. The steak had been painted garishly, like a carney attraction. The bone in the middle stared at you like a killer's eyeball.

EAT IT ALL AND YOU DON'T PAY!!!

It was implied that I was gonna have to eat a four-plus pound steak. I knew my Old Man didn't have any money.

We got there as snow began fallin'. The parkin' lot was full of zombies, trundling out of the steakhouse in a glassy-eyed daze. Barrel-gutted, toothpick-rollin', burpin', flatulent, chunderous Tennessee peckerwoods, clutchin' at their gigantic belt-buckles as if they were retaining walls. There were wives and girlfriends and buzz-headed kids in tow and the look on their faces clearly revealed heroic defeat to the Monster Rib-Eye. I didn't want to get out of the Bonneville. My Old Man called me a pussy until I gave in.

Inside, a waitress in a Santa hat took a fancy to me. Even at eight I was a bit of a heart-throb. She winked at me and suggested a twelve-ounce sirloin. But my Old Man wouldn't hear it.

'We're here for the seventy-two-ouncer,' he announced. 'Wipe its ass, chop off its legs, and plop it on a platter.'

The steaks arrived, flanked by a couch-sized baked potato and roughly a quarter acre of salad. The waitress slid two platters on to the table with an even-handed flourish. 'Good luck,' she said. The Old Man carved into his with go-for-broke zeal, prodding his fork into the rib-eye's sides, inspectin' it for excess fat like a livestock auctioneer. He watched me with one eye zipped tightly closed.

'Pace yerself, son,' he said. 'Otherwise it's gonna whip you.'

I knew I was never gonna get through it. It was as big and tenderless as a baseball glove.

The Old Man kept goin' at his, chewin' and chewin' until his face began to lose all expression. He looked like a cow, gnawin' blankly into space. It might have been the only project he ever completed in his whole life. When he'd put the last bite into his mouth, he stood up and announced it weakly to the room. There was a smattering of applause and he ceremoniously undid his belt buckle and unloaded a belch that visibly moved the hair of several nearby diners.

He sat back down and urged me on.

'Once you're halfway through it,' he said, 'you're gambling with *their* money.'

My gut was as tight as a cantaloupe. I couldn't breathe without pain. But he just kept pushin' me on.

'C'mon big man. C'mon big man. C'mon big man,' over and over.

Somethin' in his whiskey-soaked reasonin' had decided this was a rite of passage for me. One by one, the other diners cleared out until we were alone in the middle of the room. By now, the waitresses were glowerin' at us and a busboy had stacked every chair but ours upside down on to the tables, making a roomful of antlers. I started cryin', but not from humiliation. I thought it might free up some space.

'C'mon big man.'

By the end, he was on top of me, stuffin' forkfuls into my mouth while I tried to slide under the table. The waitress tried to take pity, told him it was okay, we didn't have to pay. But he kicked at her like a mustang until she retreated to the kitchen.

When I got the last bite down he slapped me on the shoulder and gave out a whoop.

'That's my boy!' he shouted. 'I believe,' he called out to the waitress, 'business is done here!'

*   *   *

172

I staggered out the door and collapsed on to the parkin' lot gravel. The Old Man dragged me by an arm to the car. We peeled out of the parkin' lot, that old Bonneville spittin' snow and gravel, headin' home. I lay across the front seat and felt every curve in that road stretchin' at my insides. I wanted to die and take my Old Man with me. His gut, basketball shaped, was now wedged against the steerin' wheel. I reached over to my side of the bench seat, found the electric seat button and pushed it.

At first, he might've thought the car was shrinkin' around him. The steerin' wheel constricted his gut, pythonlike, and his arms spread forward like emerging wings.

'Fuck's wrong with this sumbitchin' steerin' wheel?' he muttered.

Then he figured it out and made a desperate grab across the seat for my wrist, but I had him trapped. I didn't care if we crashed or not.

Finally, he slid the car to a stop and fought for the button at his own side, but I held mine steadfast. The seat motor whined in a stalemate. His eyes bulged and his face turned crimson and suddenly he exploded, rib-eye and trimmings splatterin' across the Bonneville's dashboard in lumpy technicolor glory. There was a tree-shaped air-freshener hangin' from the rear-view mirror and now it was festooned with bits of digested salad for garland. It was the closest we would ever come to havin' a Christmas tree. I pushed the car door open, rolled out and straight down a snowy embankment. Then I lay there, starin' up at the fallin' flakes until I heard the car pull away.

And that was one of the *nicest* things he ever did for me.

I got home to the trailer in Wartburg. Brenda and Althea were at the kitchen table. *The Jungle Book* was playin' on the stereo. That was all she listened to anymore.

'Look what the cat dragged in,' said Althea with her usual spry wit.

I went straight into the bedroom and came out with a gym bag packed with clothes.

'I need to talk to you,' I said to Brenda.

'Looks like someone's cuttin' out,' Althea muttered.

'I got to go see my Old Man in Atlantic City,' I said. I'd barely ever mentioned him to Brenda. 'I think he's about to take the dirt nap.'

'It's clear you don't intend to take me along,' she said.

'You're in the middle of a trial,' I said.

'Not anymore. I'm dropping the charges against Tony.'

Those tryciclics had depleted her will. Any fool could see that.

'I'll be back in a week,' I said.

'No you won't,' said Althea. I ignored her.

'In the meantime,' I said to Brenda, 'I need a word of encouragement that you'll come back to life soon.'

'Brenda and I have been talkin' about gettin' her resituated,' Althea informed me. 'Your leavin' makes that a whole lot easier.'

'We'll talk about it when I get back. I ain't in my right mind now,' I said.

'As if you ever was,' said Althea.

'You,' I said to Althea, 'need to sit down to a steamin'-hot bowl of shut the fuck up.' She looked down at her fingernails and buffed them on her blouse, like she'd just won some petty fight.

'I figured all along we weren't gonna survive no real test,' Brenda said. It was the first lucid thing she'd said in months.

'I swear I'm comin' back,' I said.

174

'And when you do, her brother will be out,' said Althea. 'I'm sure he'll take a real fraternal shine to you.'

I drove through Kentucky, up toward Ohio. Comin' upon a small Northern Kentucky town where a massive gray water tower exclaimed 'Florence, Y'all', I hit the first swarm of cicadas. It looked like a low condensed rain cloud, racin' headlong toward the windshield. Then there was a steady pop, pop, pop, of hard carcasses against the car. The windshield turned to mustard and hot-dog relish. Other cars on the road had slowed to a funeral-procession crawl, the faces of the drivers shit-scared, yellowish-looking from the color that had taken over the sky. The bugs were gettin' into the engine through the Falcon's grill and I could feel the carburetor coughin'. Finally, the Falcon gave up and I lurched it to the side of the highway.

I got out and wrestled the hood open. The cicadas were ping-pongin' off of me, stinging my face and arms – droning motorized bullets. They peppered the engine block, writhin' in a grisly tableau of barbecued agony. They made me think of the first time I'd met George Lively in all his bug-infested glory. Maybe the Sahara had paid out for him and he was sittin' at a Vegas poker table now, drinking bourbon, so right angled he could read the next player's hand.

The Falcon's carburetor was clogged. There was nothin' to do but get back in the car and wait out the barrage. When it ended, the entire highway was spackled in gore. I got out and crunched through the carnage on foot, a half mile or so to a truckstop.

I had an AAA card that I'd once found in a wallet under the bleachers at a donkey basketball game. The card was in the name of Dr Sydney Perlmutter. I'd kept the AAA card,

175

the money, a PADI diving card, and two VIP gold membership cards to Nashville titty bars – The Palomino and The Silver Saddle. Everything else, I'd mailed back to the address on the driver's license. Even a Good Samaritan deserves a finder's fee.

I called the road service on a pay phone, told 'em I was Dr Syd Perlmutter and where I'd broken down. The voice on the other end seemed to take pleasure in informin' me it would be several hours.

'Northern Kentucky is under aerial attack,' the voice announced, like Orson Welles.

I hoofed it back to my car. By now it was dark. I sat in the Falcon and listened to the radio, the local Florence station. The DJ kept interruptin' *Classic Oldies* to pinpoint the location of the next bug blitzkrieg. You could detect a new-found civic authority in his voice. It probably beat the hell out of spinnin' old Cheap Trick hits.

Another swarm of cicadas passed through. In the darkness it sounded like pebbles hittin' a steel barrel.

Suddenly, the headlights of a rescue truck reeled through the back window. I got out to meet the driver. Two flannel-shirted good ol' boys came right up to me, lookin' particularly excited. I knew somethin' wasn't right because road rescue guys ain't known for their brisk demeanor.

'Where's Dr Perlmutter?' asked one. I was wearin' a sleeveless T-shirt with Bob Seger on it and one of my cowboy boots was wrapped in silver duct tape to keep it from disintegrating. Bearin' this in mind, I made myself sound as doctorly as possible.

'Yes. That would be me.'

'What kinda doctor are you?' asked the other one, all business.

'I am the Chief Resident Neurologist at Vanderbilt University Hospital.'

'Zattafact?' said the serious one. 'That mean you know CPR?'

'Pioneered it, why?'

'We gotta fella up the road hurt bad, we're all thinkin' heart attack. Come with us.'

I wanted to tell them I had to chair an important seminar on motor neuron disease in Cincinnati, but they practically frogmarched me to the truck and shoved me in between them. We spun around and drove the wrong way up the interstate maybe a quarter mile. Another rescue truck was parked broadside on the shoulder. Flashlight beams danced out of a ditch by the roadside and I could make out the upturned chassis of a car, its wheels splayed like a hapless upended turtle.

We climbed out of the truck, down the embankment, and I saw a businessman lyin' a few feet away from the car. Whether he'd been hurled or dragged away from the car, I couldn't tell. But he didn't look too good. A rescue mechanic was kneelin' over him, wishin' for all the world he had a reference manual for this make and model.

'Give way!' yelled one of the rescue guys. 'This here's a doctor.'

'Do your stuff,' the other mechanic said to me.

And I did. I didn't know the first goddamn thing about cardiopulmonary resuscitation. I stood there frozen for a moment, feelin' the weight of expectancy on my back. All I knew was the Heimlich maneuver. So I got behind the guy, lifted him up and threw everything I had into him. I knew it was useless, but I had to at least look like I knew what I was doin'.

Astonishingly, the man ejected a hard brown husk, a cicada three inches long. Minutes later he was shakin' hands all around. The road boys pointed me out as his savior. He hugged me and I told him it was what any ordinary decent guy would've done.

*　　*　　*

Simpson's Motel sat on the Old Atlantic City Highway, flexin' old pink and green neon, tryin' to convince the world it still mattered. At the front desk, the manager, an emaciated version of Steve McQueen, emerged from a small room. I could make out a daybed behind him. 'What a fuckin' life', I thought. Confined to a shittier room than the ones you rent out. I told him who I was there to see. We chatted for a few minutes, then he gave me a key to Room 22.

I knocked and no one answered. Knocked again. Then, I let myself in. A familiar smell came back to me. Whiskey. Cigarettes. Brylcreme. A TV, no program, just surf, made the only light in the room.

My Old Man sat hunched over a wooden writin' desk, his back to me, smoke curlin' from a cigarette gripped fiercely in his teeth. Through the swirl I could make out his impossible pompadour, a great silver ship comin' out of the fog. It swung around and there was that face, that sozzled, wily, zipper-eyed, codgery sonofabitchin' face that hadn't even bothered to watch me come into the world, preferrin' instead a Dodgers–Yankee matchup on a TV in a Knoxville tavern.

'Took yer own time showin' up,' he said. He was wearin' pajamas. There was a tube of cement in his hand and he seemed to be repairin' somethin'.

'Fella at the desk asked me to talk some sense into you in the way of towels and bedsheets,' I said. 'Say's you been stonewallin' the maid for three weeks running.'

'The maids don't wanna see what I'm doin' to their linen,' he replied, and turned back to whatever he was repairin'. 'I leak like a lawn sprinkler.'

'Shouldn't you be in the hospital?'

'I already been,' he snapped. 'You want some whiskey?'

'No thanks.'

178

'Well don't just stand there with your dick in yer hand. Sit somewhere.'

I took a seat on the edge of the bed. He took a drag on his cigarette and swung his chair around to face me.

'They put a balloon in my portal vein,' he said, trailin' a shaky finger across his gut. 'Supposed to divert blood to the liver.' He stared disgustedly at his stomach, like it was glass and he could see the pointless inner workings.

'You believe that?' he said. 'A *balloon*? Like it was my birthday party.' He took a gulp from a plastic cup, then waited as he always did, for the whiskey to swim to his toes. I looked around the room. Empty Fritos bags, whiskey bottles and outdoor magazines. When he was gone, there wasn't gonna be much to his life a maid couldn't erase in an hour or so.

'Doctor said it was as much as he can do. Anyone could see they'd already written me off as a horse who ain't gonna finish. So I grabbed some Demerol, some ephedrine and a handy little forceps-type deal that's perfect for crackin' open crab legs, and left right by the admittin' desk. Didn't nobody say boo to me.'

'They musta told you stop drinkin',' I said.

'Specifically, the doc said to lay off the Jack Daniel's.' He swirled his cup around and grinned that cagey grin of his. 'So I've switched to Johnnie Walker.'

From the next room, I could hear a screamin' couple, muffled threats, lumber splittin' and what sounded like a yelpin' chihuahua caught in the middle. Christ, my whole fuckin' life was walls too flimsy or too thick. Plywood or prison. One of these days, I thought, I'm gonna have me a place made from proper two-by-fours, with proper fuckin' insulation between the walls so I ain't gotta hear other people's lives bleedin' through the goddamned walls.

'What'd you go up for at Brushy?' he asked.

'Aaah. Stealin' trailers.'

'Ambitious.'

'Well, I've straightened up. I'm singin' now.'

'You don't say. You?'

'Yep. Writin' songs. Gettin' up on stage.'

'What would put that in yer head?'

'It's a proper livin'. No heavy liftin'. Sleep late.'

'What do you know,' he mused. We sat there, quiet. I couldn't think of much else worth mentionin' from the last ten years. There wasn't no point in talkin' about crime, or my joint at Brushy, or three fucked-up marriages, or savin' some guy's life on the way up here.

'What are you workin' on there?' I finally asked.

'Building a model ship,' he replied. Spread across the table in front of him were various plastic parts in disarray. The skeleton of a small sailin' vessel was propped against a mirror. Beside that, a soldering gun and a large tomato-juice can, stripped of its label. It was weird to imagine my Old Man as an enthusiast of anything so trivial. Maybe he was in his second childhood.

'That some kind of physical therapy?' I asked.

'This,' he said, holdin' up the can, 'is my legacy.' He held it to his ear and shook it, rattlin' the contents.

'Hear that? That's the *Cutty Sark*. Perfect in every detail.'

'Where?'

'Inside the can, dumbshit. Here.' He handed it to me. I could feel *somethin'* in there. The lid had been soldered back in place.

'You're buildin' ships in cans?' I said.

'Painstakingly detailed.'

'I thought people built ships in bottles.'

'People who don't have the shakes build ships in bottles. I prefer cans.'

180

I gave it back to him. 'Well, it certainly *feels* seaworthy,' I said. It was becomin' apparent he was delirious.

'Keep it. It's yours. I been waitin' for you to show up. You bring any money?'

'I got about four hundred dollars,' I said, 'but I ain't givin' it to you to pour down your gullet.'

He ignored me. Instead, he rose and padded into the bathroom, lookin' curved and misshapen. Even stooped over, his pompadour still brushed the overhead jamb of the bathroom doorway. He stood over the toilet and peed in agony. Chambers, membranes, bulkheads and walls must've all been collapsin' inside him the way he howled. I waited for the sound of a flush and when it finally cleared, I heard him sigh with relief.

'Your momma,' he said, his back still to me, 'was somethin' else. Perfectly symmetrical. Backside like one of them gibbons. And the same exact width as her bosoms.'

I waited, wondrin' where he was goin' with this.

'Her best feature.'

'You're talkin' about my momma,' I said. 'You ought to say somethin' more respectful than that.'

'It's what I remember. At night I dream of soft nudes, figureheads on the front of a ship. They all have your momma's face on them.'

He trudged back into the bedroom and stood in front of me.

'Listen carefully. I have made arrangements to be cremated. The ashes are to be divided mutually. Half in an urn which I want delivered to your momma. She can put it up on her knicknack shelf beside all them spoons from round the world she likes to collect. The other half, I want you to put into that ship-in-the-can I gave you and thrown over the pier at Ventnor Beach, which is south of here, though not quite as the crow flies.'

181

'You want your ashes thrown out to sea?'

'Exactly.'

'Why?'

He lowered himself fraily on to his chair. 'I never seen the ocean till I got here. Now I cain't seem to stop lookin' at it. I intend to cross it.'

I told him he wasn't gonna get very far. Probably wash up south of here near some Delaware oil refinery.

'Well, you don't know much about the Gulf Stream do you?' he barked. 'By my calculations I'll reach the Ivory Coast, where some curious native youngster will find me, empty my contents on to a beach and take delight in playin' with his new-found toy.'

'Assumin' he has a can opener,' I said.

The Old Man stared at me humorlessly.

'It ain't like you to get this sudden romanticism,' I said. 'Why do you want to be cremated?'

'I don't need to go into the details,' he explained, 'but in so many words, I've sold the rights to my cadaver.'

'What are you talkin' about?'

'A Mortuary Science school. Here in town. They advanced me the money. When I'm officially dead, they get to carve into me like a laboratory frog.'

I shook my head.

'I needed the money,' he said, sheepishly. 'But now I'm havin' serious misgivings.'

He poured himself another dollop of whiskey into the cup, then reluctantly offered the bottle my way.

'No thanks. How much did they pay you?'

'Who?'

'The mortuary school.'

'Which one?'

'There's more than one?'

'Yeah.'

'How many?'

He didn't answer.

'How many times *have* you sold your body?!'

'Five.'

'Five *different* mortuary schools?'

'One's a cosmetics company,' he answered, lookin' distraught.

'Christ, they're gonna be scrappin' over you like dogs at a T-bone.'

'I don't intend to give any of 'em the satisfaction. So I went through the Yellow Pages and found a fella over in Toms River agreed to do a complete cremation for $999.95. I'd appreciate it if you'd oversee the deal.'

'You ain't dead yet.'

'I will be soon's I get my hands on $999.95.'

'You could come back to Tennessee with me,' I said. 'I'll look after you. Help you dry out.'

'Oh, I'm gonna dry out alright.'

'You don't hafta do this.'

'I don't see no way out,' he said. 'Look at this.' He rolled up a pajama leg to reveal a thick black plastic band on his ankle.'They put an elk tag on me.'

'Who did that?'

'The mortuary school.'

'*Which* mortuary school!'

'I don't quite remember.'

'That ain't right,' I said. 'That's fuckin' illegal. And inhuman.'

'Well, you don't understand how things are done in Atlantic City, do you, shitforbrains?' he said bitterly. 'We're not exactly dealin' with the most ethical teaching institutions.'

He reached into a desk drawer, fished out a clump of bills and threw it on the bed beside me.

'That's about a hunnert dollars, right there. I reckon we should put that with your four hunnert and go double it at a roulette table. Red or black, one spin.'

'You're crazy.'

'If we double our money, you get me cremated. If we lose, I'll come back to Tennessee with you.'

I thought about it.

'Black,' I finally said.

'Red,' he replied.

I helped the Old Man get dressed for the trip to the casino. He delicately eased himself into some loose-cut Wranglers, a striped Western shirt with diamond-shaped buttons and cowboy boots – pumice-colored Tony Llamas that looked like they'd been rebuilt a half dozen times. He checked his pompadour in the mirror, made sure it was rigid, then I walked him out to my car. He refused to lean on my arm.

It was late evenin' and all along the coastal plain you could see the casinos lit up like luminous weddin' cakes. The Old Man told me he was partial to one called Claridges. He pointed to it in the distance and I steered the Falcon in that direction. It was a depressin' place, Atlantic City. Figures, hunched over, skirted through the broken glass and upheaved sidewalks, buried in hooded sweatshirts even though it was a hot summer night. Everywhere there were hollow buildings bandaged with plywood.

We drove by a department store called Two Guys and in the parkin' lot, climbing behind the wheel of a Chevrolet Vega, I saw Dolly Parton. I recognized the pout, the beauty mark, the big explosion of blondness.

'Fuck me,' I said to the Old Man, 'I just seen Dolly Parton.'

'The hell you did,' he said.

'I'm not lyin'. Gettin' into a Chevy.'

'Why would Dolly Parton be in a Chevy?'

'I don't know. But it sure as hell looked like her.'

We got to the edge of a vast parkin' area surroundin' Claridges and had to leave the car and wait to transfer to a shuttle bus, like in a hostage drama. The bus stop was full of sullen, bulbous, big-pored troglodytes, clutchin' plastic cups full of dirty nickels to their chests. 'Christ,' I thought to myself, 'this is the ugliest parade of human rodentia I've ever seen.' And I'm from Tennessee.

I figured that must be why the Miss America pageant is held here. So that once a year they can trundle in fifty-odd beautiful gals to remind everyone in Atlantic City there are actually some good-lookin' people in the world.

The Old Man hobbled on to the bus, informin' the driver his pecker-headed son claimed to have just seen Dolly Parton.

The bus driver shrugged and let the weary sigh of the bus's hydraulic doors answer for him. We took a seat. The ride to the casino entrance was punctuated with quick annoyed exchanges among impatient passengers.

'Lean back, I can't see out,' someone behind us said.

'There's nothin' to see. It looks like Dresden.'

'Give me the VapoRub.'

'Why? What is it?'

'Just give me the goddamned VapoRub.'

'My left hand is itchin'. That's a good sign.'

'Look. Vic Damone at the Sands. Ever tell you about the time I met him? In the service?'

'Yeah, about a thousand times you told me that.'

'Gimme the VapoRub!'

My Old Man appeared to fall asleep during the brief ride. I studied his face – spidery veins and spongy nose – and tried to imagine how he had ended up in Atlantic City.

Abruptly, he opened his eyes and caught me starin' at him.

'You want some Johnnie Walker?' he asked, reaching for the bottle in his hip.

'No thanks. I'm an Old Grand-Dad man.'

He unscrewed the cap and shook his head disconsolately.

'I suppose it's wrong for a dad to expect his son to live up to certain expectations. But I guess I always hoped you'd grow up to be a whiskey man, not a bourbon man. You're breakin' my heart, y'know.'

'Sorry,' I said. 'I like bourbon.'

'Kentucky horsepiss. Tit syrup.'

The bus arrived at the casino entrance and disgorged us. The Old Man shuffled into the lobby and every doorman and bell-hop there knew him.

'How are ya, J.D.?'

'I'm alright, Jose. How's it hangin'?'

'Evening, J.D.'

'Hiya, Frank, say hello to my boy, Otis.' Everywhere, heads turned to admire or recoil from his pompadour.

Instead of goin' straight to the roulette table, the Old Man made a wide foray around the edge of the huge casino. He wasn't shufflin' anymore. He walked like he owned the place. I hadn't never been in a casino before and I was amazed by the din. I never knew money could be so loud. Everywhere, you could hear it clangin' against metal like a million crashin' beer bottles. No one seemed to be talkin' – they were all too intent on winnin' money. At the blackjack table, people spoke with their hands, a wave for no, a tap for yes. A craps winner in a blue leisure suit suddenly bounded like a cheerleader, joy bubbling from his throat. No one around him seemed to give a shit.

We reached a long cocktail bar where a few drinkers perched on stools, idly feedin' quarters into the electronic poker machines imbedded into the counter. I watched my

186

Old Man perform what was obviously a well-practiced routine. He went up to each poker machine and systematically fished underneath where the coin reject slot was. They were hidden from view and I reckon most of the players didn't even know they were there. By the time he'd covered the length of the bar the Old Man had a fistful of rejected quarters. I realized then, this was how he got by day to day. The bartenders didn't seem to mind. It was that pompadour of his. It commanded some kind of mutant respect.

We took a seat at the bar. He stacked the quarters on the countertop and ordered himself a Johnnie Walker Black, neat. When it arrived he took a long time savoring it. Then he talked into his glass.

'I know you think I'm a no-count, no-good bastard,' he said.

'What I think is *professional loner* suits you.'

'I do better detached,' he answered, and I couldn't feel any resentment about that.

'Back when you was just a tiny ankle-biter,' he said, 'your grandaddy surveyed land for the Bank of Knoxville. You didn't know that, did you?'

'No, I didn't.'

'Yepper. Appraised farm property. He'd have to walk off the dimensions, check for jimson weed and ox-eye.'

'I can't see him workin' for a bank. But I can see the noxious weed part of it.'

'There was this couple up in Bristol wanted to buy an old farmstead. The bank sent him out there with a deed to survey it. Beautiful little spread with a nice red house and a porch that looked out forever. All the boundaries was marked by natural landmarks – trees and boulders and whatall. The deed said 'bordered on the south by a creek'. But it was drawn up way back in 1837 and he could tell that creek had shifted considerably since then, in favor of the couple. Maybe an extra five acres. Now Daddy had some money set aside, hid under floorboards in the kitchen, and figured to buy that place himself.'

'Why didn't he put the money in the bank?'

'Shysters, ev'ry last one of 'em! Hell, they had *him* workin' for 'em! The three of us, Momma, him and me, was livin' in a cold-water flat. It would've been the grandest thing he ever did, a farm to call our own. But he needed twice the money he had for a down payment. He went to the bank and instructed 'em not to approve that couple's loan, said the land was ruint by spurge and knapweed. Then he come home, took that cash outta the floorboards and went over to the Brown Proctor Hotel, where they used to run gamblin' and whores outta the fifth floor. Poker, craps, horses, roulette, you name it. He went up to the roulette table, plopped down the wad and told the wheelman to let it ride on red, the color of the farmhouse. And he spun that wheel and it come up black. Black as a telephone. Black as fuckin' black can be. Your grandaddy had to come home and tell my momma what he'd done and she called him the foolest man God had ever set on this earth. Bundled me up and took off to her momma's. Daddy had to beg her to come back.'

'Momma never told me nothin' about that,' I said.

'Nah, I don't reckon she'd of been inclined. But if that ball had landed on red, we'd neither of us be sittin' here right now. Turns out that creek was full of sapphires the size of walnuts. You drive up there now, it's still bein' mined.'

He went all quiet, probably envisionin' a life as a sapphire king, Tennessee cracker nobility.

Then he pushed a crooked finger in to my chest.

'Now, I reckon, by odds, the wheel is on our side this time.' With that, he hoisted himself off the stool, swept up his whiskey glass and headed for the roulette table. I followed him, thinkin' I ought to exert some kind of control over the misguided sonofabitch. At the very least, get him back in the hospital to dry out. But I knew it wouldn't do no good. He was hell-bent on finishin' himself and he was gonna make sure it was with a flourish.

The roulette table was bustlin'. He gingerly placed himself on the corner seat nearest the wheelman and pulled the wad of money from his pocket. Directly behind us, a soul trio in matchin' pale-green suits performed to an empty lounge. A half dozen white musicians crowded the stage behind them. The lead singer, whose hair appeared laminated, was extemporizing on 'If You Don't Know Me By Now'.

Baby, I done tried my best. But you walked across my heart in golf cleats. And now you're out alleycattin' with my best friend. I just cain't do this no more . . . baby, baby, baby . . .

The two back-up singers dip, dip, dipped along, wondrin' just how much emotion to invest in a room of empty seats. Suddenly the lead singer announced he was 'gonna leave this song alone' and left the horn section stranded, soundin' like snarled traffic.

The Old Man rubbed his money back and forth across the tabletop nervously, like he didn't want it to leave his fingers. He was lookin' around for the cocktail waitress.

'I need a good-luck drink,' he said.

We waited for a waitress who eventually appeared at the Old Man's side. The Old Man gave her a salty once over and ordered a Johnnie Walker Black, neat.

'Whaddyll y'have?' he asked me, then added, conspiratorially, 'Well, drinks is free.'

'Free?'

'If you're gamblin' they're free.'

No wonder he'd come to Atlantic City.

The wheelman was gettin' impatient waitin' for my Old Man to make a move.

'Play or don't stay,' he said sharply.

'Put it on black,' I said to the Old Man. Somethin' inside me was screamin' black. I ain't psychic, but I *just felt* it.

I said it again. 'Put it on black, Daddy.'

He looked right at me.

'You ain't never called me *Daddy*.' He said it like all the hardness in his soul had just evaporated. If there was ever any bridge between us, any filament lent by the mysterious, fucked-up gene pool the two of us shared, this was it.

He shoved the money toward the wheelman.

'Pay no mind to my dumbass kid. Put it all on red,' he said loudly, making sure everyone heard him. For that brief instant he was a cattle baron, a tycoon, a real high roller. The wheelman shrugged, plopped the money down on the red field and pinned it with a weight.

Then he spun the wheel. At the same moment the waitress returned with the drink.

'Johnnie Walker Red . . .' she said, putting it down in front of the Old Man.

The Old Man flinched. 'Black not Red!!' he shouted.

The waitress's eyes flashed with anger at my Old Man's abruptness. The wheelman never looked up. He just heard my Old Man yell 'black not red!!' and moved the wad of money on to the black space.

'Whatthefuckyoudoin'?' the Old Man yelled.

'You just said black!' said the wheelman.

'I meant the Johnnie Walker!' The Old Man came up off his stool. He lurched for his money, but the wheelman pushed his arm away.

'Too late,' he said. 'Your money's on black.'

The roulette ball clattered in the wheel and came to a stop. Twenty-nine. Black.

Everyone at the table seemed startled and confused.

'I'll be a sonofabitch,' said the Old Man. He knocked back his drink with one gulp and cackled.

'Get the chips from the gentleman,' he said to me and staggered away from the table. 'I gotta take a piss!'

I walked over to the cage to cash in the thousand dollars' worth of chips. There was a showroom next to it where a straggle of audience members had taken their seats, waitin' listlessly for whatever sub-par extravaganza the casino was throwin' their way.

With a fanfare, the curtain came up and there was Dolly Parton standin' at the microphone. A band kicked into *Jolene* and the crowd clapped torpidly.

It wasn't Dolly, of course. The banner behind her read 'Legends of Country' and listed an historically improbable lineup: Dolly Parton, Hank Williams, Willie Nelson, Buddy Holly and, for some inexplicable reason, Jim Morrison.

Still, I was mesmerized by her. Not by her voice, but by the twin assets that had surely won her the audition in the first place. Her outfit was a masterstroke of redneck kinkiness – a gingham bodice so tight she looked like she was crawling out of an apple core. Wisely, the producers had realized that a plummeting cleavage was a perfect decoy for a voice that sounded like an electric tin-opener.

I couldn't take my eyes off her.

I walked over to one of the lounge tables and picked up a table tent that explained the show and listed the cast's names. Dolly Parton was Brenda Tuttle.

Brenda Tuttle.

'This,' I thought to myself, 'is gettin' ridiculous.'

*   *   *

'The deal was I win, I get my cremation!' my Old Man argued. He was drunk now and lyin' in a craps table, arms across his chest, imaginin' himself in a spacious felt-lined casket.

'Climb outta the craps table will you, Daddy?'

'Stop callin' me Daddy. It sounds goddamn weird.'

'Come on.'

'Not until you agree to oversee my cremation. I'm warnin' you, I can die right here.'

'It was a fluke. You picked red. It came up black.'

'I won, didn't I?'

'You won the money. But you *lost* the bet.'

'I didn't lose the bet. I got a grand in my pocket. How did I lose the bet?'

It was an insane argument but I didn't want to give in. There must've been *somethin'* a grand could do for you in the hospital. A down payment on a new liver, maybe. I wasn't sure. But I was determined not to see my Old Man turned into a floatin' ashtray.

A security guard came over and peered into the table.

'What's the problem here?' he said.

'It's my Old Man. He's being dramatic.'

'Oh, it's you J.D.,' the security guard said, like this was the most normal thing in the world. 'You alright?'

'Yeah, Julius is it?'

'Jules.'

'Jules, could you get me a glass of water?'

'Sure thing.'

'With some Johnnie Walker Black in it?'

'I'll see what I can do.' The guard went off.

'Now lissen up, son, to what I'm tellin' you. Temptation will pay for itself in physical attrition. I've drunk too much, abused myself thoroughly and taken a fidelitous misstep or two. Once, a boyfriend of a woman I knew chased me down

192

a stairwell with a pickax.' He paused, probably replayin' that particular antic in his mind.

'And the handmaiden to this kind of behavior is Guilt, great big peptic heaps of it. You followin' me, here?'

'Sort of.'

'Well, you better 'cause this is my deathbed confession. It's been one lie after another. Small ones, big ones, epic ones with plot twists as preposterous as them 007 films.' Awkwardly, he sat up in the middle of the table.

'And one Great Lie, an Umbrella Lie to cover 'em all . . .' With that, he brought his hands to his pompadour and carefully lifted it off his head, as if he were removin' a fragile nest from the crook of a tree. He set the wig down on the felt table surface and ran a faltering hand across his naked head.

'This is what has separated me from a common wino and scrounger,' he said.

I fuckin' couldn't believe it. All those years, putting Brylcreme on a *wig*.

'You used to go to a *barber* every week!' I said.

'Decent enough fella. Knew to keep his mouth shut. For that, I don't resent him runnin' off with your momma.'

He closed his eyes and laid his head back on the table's burled edge.

'Where the fuck's that drink?' he said, then passed away.

Brenda #4

What can I tell you about my fourth wife? Loyal. Tits like a dead heat in a zeppelin race. Perfectly turned calves and fragrant as the interior of a new truck. Sometimes I could hardly believe my own luck, the way we just settled in together, effortlessly.

And when she put her eyes on and her caky make-up, penciled a beauty mark on to her cheek and lowered that great billowing blonde wig on to her head, she was my other wife, Miss Dolly Parton. To be married to two different women seemed to me a thunderous achievement.

She made me gloriously happy. Unfortunately, that's pretty much all I can tell you about the two years we were married 'cause I stayed drunk the whole time. I'd met her thirty minutes after my Old Man kicked the bucket, after they'd wheeled him out of the casino. He knocked me for a loop in one direction; she knocked me in the other. When you get hit with a combination like that, your best defense is a negotiated retreat to any bottle with old-timey-style writin' on the label. 'Cause that's the place where time stands still.

When I'm drunk, I can appreciate the rarity of domestic

bliss, the wondrous hum of mundane daily life, the small-but-necessary delusions plain ordinary couples labor under just to keep goin'.

But at some point, you gotta sober up.

Cold Flame

I'm underneath the kitchen sink of an apartment in Ventnor, New Jersey. The real-estate people called it a garden apartment when Brenda #4 and me moved in. That don't mean it has a garden because it doesn't. It just means all the apartments look out over a communal lawn, which, as far as I can tell, has never seen the shadow of the 'full-time gardener on premises' the agent promised. The grass and weeds are overgrown, makin' it a mouse haven, and now the mice have moved inside. Which is why I'm under the sink with a dollop of peanut butter and a mousetrap. I'm goin' to nail this little rodent if it's the only thing I do all day – which it is. That and not drink. Those are my projects for the day.

It won't be hard not to drink because Brenda #4 locks me in the house when she goes off to work. I made her put a six-inch Master padlock on the outside of the front door. It's the only way in and out, unless I'm desperate enough to climb over the rear balcony and jump fifteen feet like I've just shot Lincoln.

I am, effectively, a prisoner in the Ocean Breeze Garden Apartment Complex, livin' out my own *Days of Wine and Roses*.

It's for my own good. Believe me, I haven't been the most sociable person since I quit drinkin'. When I'm allowed out of the apartment, that is, when Brenda #4 *takes* me out, I have a tendency to be surly to everyone. Just the other day I went alongside her to the Shoprite, the local supermarket. We had the shoppin' cart packed to the rim and were waitin' in the checkout line. There was a frail old lady behind me with just a carton of milk. She had a mewly look on her face, clearly meant to indicate that any decent human should let her ahead in line. My wife didn't notice, she was busy readin' a soap-opera digest from the magazine rack. I turned to the lady and politely said, 'Is that all you have, just milk?'

'Yes it is,' she replied, meekly.

'Well then,' I said, cheerfully, 'you need to go buy a shit-load more stuff 'cause we're gonna be here quite a while!'

It's the dryin'-out business that makes me like this, like I'm bein' pushed downhill in a barrel of barbed wire. I can *feel* the inside of my skin and it's like a raw seepin' blister.

Twice a week I go to a doctor. I'm not even sure what kind of doctor he is – I never asked. I met him at a bar a few months back. One night, shitfaced, I asked him if he could get me Ant-Abuse and he gave me his card and told me to come see him in the daytime. Now he's sort of my crutch and confidant. He keeps an office over on Margate Avenue, a little cubbyhole of a place with no receptionist and a Coke machine in the ante-room. Sometimes I get the feelin' I'm his only patient.

'You stayin' dry?' he says. I'm sittin' across from his desk.

'Yeah,' I answer. 'When does it start to feel normal?'

'When you start doin' normal things,' he says. He blows a big plume of cigarette smoke into the air as if that's his final word on the subject. It doesn't worry me much that he's a three-carton-a-day doctor. I asked him once how, in the interest of medical ethics, he could be a chain-smoker.

'There's a Hippocratic oath and a hypocritic oath,' he answered, his idea of a real corker.

'What's normal?' I say, thinkin' that normal means borin', and my greatest fear is boredom.

'Normal.' He pushes his fingers together, prayer like. 'As in, take in a casino show or a movie. And buy a big bucket of popcorn. Play some miniature golf. Go fishin'. You've got to get used to the idea that life is generally a string of mundane events interrupted occasionally by something that blows a little dust up your skirt. You want more Ant-Abuse?'

'Nah, I'm fine.'

'Do what you have to do, but stop broodin' about your father's death. You've got to be positive, keep a mental image of yourself sober. I ever tell you about Art Peplo?'

'Who?'

'Art Peplo. A patient of mine, clocked in at six hundred and twenty pounds. No matter what he did, the fat bastard couldn't stop stuffin' his face. I used to have to make house calls to see him, 'cause he was so ass-heavy he couldn't get through his own front door. One day I said to him, "Art, what do you really want?" Of course, he answered, "A sixteen-inch pizza." I said, "No, what do you *really* want?" And he said, "Doc, I wanna go outside. I wanna see the blue sky and smell the fresh-mown grass." And I said, "Then *picture* yourself outside. Project beyond losin' weight. Keep that mental image in your head of standin' in your own front yard, smellin' the grass."'

'And?'

'Six months later he was standin' in his front yard.'

'That's amazin',' I say.

'Not really. His brother brought a chainsaw over and widened the doorway. But the point is, keep a clear image. You got to project yourself sober. How's the wife?'

'Never better.'

'She still doin' that lookee-likee revue?'

'Yeah.'

'That one's a keeper,' he chirps. 'Alright, I gotta let you go. I got a real patient in here at three-thirty. One with insurance coverage.'

So now I'm locked in an apartment, tryin' to project myself sober.

I haven't had a drink since the night I got in a fight with a biker at one of Brenda #4's shows. I used to love watchin' Brenda do her Dolly songs, especially 'Tennessee Homesick Blues' and 'Dagger Through the Heart'. I didn't even mind 'Nine to Five' and 'I Will Always Love You'. But then she and the Roy Orbison impersonator, Carl Valentine, would team up for 'Love Hurts', the old Orbison hit, later ruined by Cher. And every night, Brenda #4 would get the goddamn lyrics wrong.

It's supposed to go like this:

> I really learned a lot, really learned a lot
> Love is like a stove that burns you when it's hot
> Love Hurts
> Ooooooh, Love Hurts.

But in their version, Carl would sing:

> I really learned a lot, really learned a lot

And then Brenda would sing:

> Love is like a flame that burns when it's hot

And it would drive me up the fuckin' wall. So one night I said somethin' to her.

'When is a flame *not* hot?' This was after the show, when we were all sittin' around one of the lounge tables: Me, Dolly, Roy Orbison, Willie Nelson and Jim Morrison.

'What do you mean?' she said.

'I mean, you're gettin' the lyric wrong.'

'Why does it bother you so much?' she said.

'It bothers me 'cause it's such a great song.'

'Well, I'm pretty sure it wasn't written for *you*,' she said, gettin' all pouty.

Man, did that remark piss me off. Like I said, I was plastered and, to be honest, a little bit jealous. Jealous of watchin' my wife on stage every night when I couldn't get a gig anywhere on the Jersey Coast 'cause all anyone wanted to hear was the Asbury Park sound: Springsteen or Southside Johnny type stuff. That's why the crowd for Brenda's country music revue was always so tiny. No one gave a shit about country music in New Jersey.

'Well, you should sing the goddamn song the way it was written,' I said.

'Whoa, whoa!' said Carl. 'Take it easy, Otis. Have another drink.'

'I don't want another drink. There's no such thing as a cold flame.'

Carl tried to change the subject, but I wouldn't let it go. I started singin':

Love is like a flame that burns when it's hot
Love hurts
Romantic walks on the beach with some kerosene
 soaked rags.
Ouch, ouch, ouch

Bodies entwined in naked passion while a grease fire
erupts in the kitchen. Oh, oh, that smarts!

'What the hell's gotten into him?' said Jim Morrison.
'He's just drunk again,' said Brenda #4, with a sigh.

Soft candlelight dinner, oops there goes the tablecloth
Second degree burns on twenty percent of my body.
Ouchy-malouchy!

Everything was bubblin' up inside me. Right then, a hairy
guy wearin' a T-shirt that read 'Shit Happens' walked by
and catcalled to Brenda #4.
'Hey, Dolly! Nice tits!'
So I got up, followed the guy out of the lounge and
cornered him by a slot machine. I said somethin' to him like:
'It's true what your shirt says, fella. "Shit" does "happen".
But fate did not make you an asshole. You did that all by
yourself.'
Then he 'happened' to kick the 'shit' out of me.
After that, Brenda #4 and me decided maybe I needed to
be quarantined.

Where once I had blue smoky mountains, Tennessee hospi-
tality, apple orchards, a good truck and Southern-style
barbecue never further than arm's length, I now have a
garden apartment with a view of vermin, nautical-theme
matchin' furniture and Brenda #4's collection of Hummel
figurines. Where once I had bourbon to keep demons at bay,
I now have a quack doctor whose idea of rehabilitation is a
bracing round of miniature golf.
I gently place the loaded mousetrap beneath the U-joint
of the kitchen sink. I'm convinced the mouse is comin' up

through the gap where the floor doesn't quite meet the wall. I slide the trap gingerly along the floor, but my fingers are shakin' so much I accidentally set it off and it snaps across my fingernail with a vicious thwack. The pain shoots straight up my arm and then I bang my head on the bottom of the sink. When my head clears, I clamber across the kitchen floor with a vitality and purpose I haven't felt in a long time. Who was it once said it's better to feel pain than to feel nothin' at all?

At that moment I hear the padlock outside bein' jiggled and then Brenda #4 walks in in a cloud of jasmine perfume and stale casino smoke. She's in her Dolly Parton get-up. She won't use the dressin' room backstage at the casino because she's the only woman in the show. Willie Nelson and Jim Morrison are always lingerin' around, waitin' for a glimpse of her tits.

'Sugar, what are you doin' down there?' she says. From this vantage point I have a great view up her skirt.

'Projectin' myself sober.'

'On my floor?' She says *her* floor, not *our* floor. Little things like that to always remind me I'm more or less livin' off her earnings.

'Things are really lookin' up!' I say. 'Ahah-hah hoo hoo hee!' That smack on the head hasn't done anything to dull my rapier wit. These days, Brenda #4 has taken to viewin' me with a pathetic tint, like a terminal patient.

'I wonder sometimes if you're missin' somethin', givin' up the drink,' she says.

'Possibly, yes. But I'm seein' things as they really are.'

I stand up and she kisses me. What a lovely gal. I can smell a trace of alcohol on her breath and it brings out my craving. I drag the kiss out as long as I can. She finally breaks it off and sits down on a kitchen chair. She extends her right leg toward me, wanting me to pull off her red cowgirl boot.

I give it a slap across the toe to loosen it, then slide it off.

I ask her how the show went this evenin', even though I already know. It's the same every night, her crowd of listless yahoos. The women will look like they've applied their make-up with a spatula. The men will have hair combed in weird contours like those high-altitude photos of South American farms. How many nights have I sat in the back of the lounge and watched idiots argue over whether or not they're watchin' the real Dolly Parton:

'I'm tellin' you that's Dolly!'

'Yeah right, and that's Jim Morrison, fresh back from the grave.'

'The show kicked serious ass tonight,' she says. That's Jerseyite for you – that harsh, flat, aggressive tone. New Jersey is always kickin' somethin's ass. Ventnor kicks Margate's ass. Margate is kickin' Red Hook's ass. Red Hook is kickin' Atlantic City's ass. *And* takin' names. That's how organized Red Hook is. When New Jersey isn't kickin' ass, it's in someone's face. Everyone has their face in someone else's face. It's a small, crowded, ass-kickin', in-your-face state.

'They're about to fire Marvin,' she mentions. Marvin is Marvin Munson, the Willie Nelson impersonator.

'They're not goin' to fire Marvin. He's the best Willie around.'

'Well, he threw another snit tonight. He's grown a catfish mustache and the producer got in his face about it.' There you go.

'Maybe he's stretchin' his character.'

'Willie Nelson doesn't have a droopy mustache. There's no two ways about that.' She extends her other boot toward me.

'To be frank, you're audience wouldn't know Willie Nelson from Nelson Mandela.'

'Whathaveyou. Anyway, the producer went ballistic.' Between ass-kickin' and interpersonal face contact, New

Jerseyites like to spend as much time as possible goin' ballistic. They're ballistic *and* in your face and, somehow, are *still* able to reach around with a leg and give you a good ass-kickin'. Believe me, it takes some real agility.

I trail her into the bedroom, followin' her curves. The gingham bodice, the big hair, Christ, it drives me crazy with lust seein' her like that. But then, as she disassembles herself, I feel it all start to fade. 'Cause this is what it's come to, our sex life: I'm only worked up when she's Dolly. When she's Brenda, nothin', zippo, Elvis leaves the buildin'.

She's not a bad-lookin' gal at all. Her real hair is an ordinary mouse brown and her face is more handsome than feminine. She's got full, pillowy lips that turn every serious thought in her head into a pout. By Atlantic City standards, not too shabby. Still, it's such a brutal letdown seein' her go from Dolly to Brenda, from prime rib to meat loaf.

She used to fuck me in the Dolly outfit but I reckon she got tired of dress-up sex and just wants to be desired for herself. And Brenda-in-the-flesh just doesn't blow dust up my skirt, to use the medical terminology.

She takes off her wig and places it delicately into a red felt-lined box, then starts takin' off the pancake mix and the beauty mark. Eventually she slips out of her gingham bodice and undoes her bra. As I watch her, I'm aware of my libido dampening like rain on a campfire. It's like some kind of reverse striptease. Then she drifts by me, runs her hand lightly across my cheek and crawls on to the bed with her ass up in the air.

'Come over here, Sugar,' she says. 'Your little kitten's had a hard day.'

That word, *sugar*, sends an encouraging surge through me. I've always wanted a gal to call me Sugar. When Brenda #4 says it, it's soft and lilting, not her Jersey voice at all – and it takes me back to Tennessee. It makes me think of bein' a child, when sugar was the supreme manifestation of Love. If someone gave you candy, you loved them – and they loved you – why else would they be givin' you candy? (Unless it was to lure you into their car.) The correlation between Love and Sugar never disappears, which is why when you love someone you think of them as a big sweet snack and call them names like *'Sugar'* or *'Honeybun'* or *'Sweetiepie'*. That's not romantic wittering, that's a scientific fact. Consult a goddamned nutritionist if you don't wanna take my word for it.

Still, this is more of an ordeal than a seduction.

I walk over to the bed and undo my belt buckle. Maybe I'll get through this. She's makin' slow, undulating circles with her hips and all the grace goes out of her right then because it looks like somethin' she picked up in a nature documentary. I push up against her, feelin' her clammy skin. I stare off at the wall, the flutterin' drapes, the lamp. I'm thinkin', 'This ain't workin', this is silly, she's *tryin' too hard* to be sexy.' I hope she isn't gonna blurt out one of those weird out-of-context porn phrases she always thinks is gonna turn me into a rutting barnyard stud. But she does.

'Shoot your poison into my wicked, wicked uterus,' she says, and backs up against me. Christ, where does she get this from? The remark brings me to a withered stop. I zip up and redo my belt buckle. These days, I don't know who I'm fuckin' anymore. A half-thought-out character somewhere between Brenda and Dolly Parton.

She doesn't move her position, just looks around at me like a cat who's not finished bein' scratched.

Then she shrugs, crawls off the bed and pads into the kitchen to warm up some meat loaf. She pouts for the rest of the evenin'.

*   *   *

206

I tell the doc I'm havin' trouble fuckin' my wife when she's my wife and not Dolly Parton.

'That's abnormal,' he says, 'but I wouldn't stress myself about it. If you met the real Dolly Parton, you probably wouldn't be able to fuck her unless she dressed up as your wife.'

'Is that a joke?'

'No, but this is. There's this shipwreck. A guy gets stranded on a desert island with Dolly Parton. After a while, they end up bangin' like crazy. This goes on for months. One day, Dolly says to him, "Is there anything you'd like me to do we haven't tried before?" The guy says, "Actually, there is. Take off your wig." She takes off her wig. He says, "Wet your hair and slick it straight back." She does like he asks. He goes over to the campfire, picks up a burnt stick and traces a mustache above her lip. Then he says, "Walk down to that end of the beach, turn around and walk back. When you get to me say, 'Hey Frank! What's new?'" She's confused, but she does like he asks. Walks down to the end of the beach, turns and comes back. She reaches the guy and says, "Hey Frank, what's new?" He shouts "What's new? I'm bangin' Dolly Parton, *that's what's new!!*"'

I stare at him.

'Is that supposed to make me feel better?'

'No, but it makes me feel better. It's a funny fuckin' joke.'

'It don't make *me* feel no better.'

'You're not tryin' to feel better, you're tryin' to feel normal.'

'I'm bored outta my fuckin' skull, Doc.'

'Boredom is normal. I've told you that.'

'But it's my biggest fear.'

I tell him about this wakin' nightmare I used to have as a kid. I would lie there and think about the Afterlife: Heaven and Hell – the version they teach in Tennessee schools. Hell was eternal fire, and Heaven was everlastin' happiness. And that phrase, *everlastin' happiness*, would send shudders through me. Whatever my current idea of happiness was – Tootsie Rolls, basketball, never havin' to go to school – I just couldn't imagine an *eternity* of it. *How* could that not get borin'? Heaven scared the hell out of me.

The doc doesn't seem to know what to say to that, so he elects to check my blood pressure, possibly to maintain a doctorly appearance. He leans over me, wraps the constrictor around my bicep and pumps away distractedly. I can smell his cigarette breath.

'Why don't you and I go fishin'?' he finally suggests. 'I got a place up on the Barnegat Inlet. Crawlin' with fluke this time of year.'

'I don't like fishin'.'

'Look,' he says, 'I can't help you if you're not gonna help yourself. Fishin' is *beneficial* to relaxation. Geddit?'

'You catch fish with these punchlines?'

He checks the blood-pressure gauge and his face gives away nothin'. 'You need to put yourself in public situations where you won't be near booze.'

'That's impossible. I'm a songwriter. I work in bars. I'm always gonna be around booze.'

'Well, you're goin' to have to figure that one out, 'cause you can't stay locked up all day. Self-imposed agoraphobia isn't the answer to your condition.'

'How's my blood pressure?'

'Your blood pressure is fine. But that's not the best indicator of stress.' He goes around his desk, opens a drawer and pulls out some charts.

'Study this.' He thrusts the chart across the desk at me.

It's somethin' called the Holmes–Rahe Life Events Scale. It lists emotional events in a person's life and assigns them 'stress units':

EVENT	STRESS UNITS
DEATH OF SPOUSE	100
DIVORCE	73
MARITAL SEPARATION	65
DEATH OF CLOSE FAMILY MEMBER	63
PERSONAL INJURY OR ILLNESS	53
MARRIAGE	50
FIRED AT WORK	47
MARITAL RECONCILIATION	45
RETIREMENT	45
CHANGE IN HEALTH OF FAMILY MEMBER	44
PREGNANCY	40
GAIN NEW FAMILY MEMBER	39
SEX DIFFICULTIES	39
BUSINESS READJUSTMENT	39
CHANGE IN FINANCIAL STATE	38
DEATH OF A CLOSE FRIEND	37
CHANGE TO DIFFERENT LINE OF WORK	36
ARGUMENT WITH SPOUSE	35
HIGH MORTGAGE	31
FORECLOSURE OF MORTGAGE OR LOAN	30
CHANGE IN RESPONSIBILITY AT WORK	29
SON OR DAUGHTER LEAVING HOME	29
TROUBLE WITH IN-LAWS	29
OUTSTANDING PERSONAL ACHIEVEMENT	28
BEGIN OR END SCHOOL	26
CHANGE IN LIVING CONDITIONS	25
REVISION OF PERSONAL HABITS	24
TROUBLE WITH BOSS	23
CHRISTMAS	12

'I've taken the liberty of circlin' the events that apply to you,' the doctor says. And he has. He's tallied up my score:

EVENT	STRESS UNITS
DEATH OF CLOSE FAMILY MEMBER	63
PERSONAL INJURY OR ILLNESS	53
CHANGE IN LIVING CONDITIONS	25
REVISION OF PERSONAL HABITS	24
TOTAL STRESS UNITS	165

'I haven't had an injury or illness,' I argue.

'You're an alcoholic, that's an illness. This shows just how misguided our perception of stress is. A guy at a nuclear plant gets reamed by his boss for spillin' radioactive waste, he's at 23. *You're* at 165. Oh, gimme that back.'

I hand the chart back to him and watch as he takes a pencil and circles: SEXUAL DIFFICULTIES: 39

'Make that 204. You're off the charts, pal. You're beyond stress. Borderin' on fission.' He gives me a serious look and leans forward for emphasis.

'So take my advice and let's go fission!' He really cracks himself up over that one.

I agree to go fishin' with the doc, provided he stops crackin' his awful jokes. He tells me to bring Brenda #4 along. She gets Monday nights off, so early in the day, we drive up the Garden State Parkway and turn right for the ocean. Barnegat Inlet separates the Jersey mainland from Long Beach, a stretch of seabreak that runs for almost fifty miles from Seaside Heights all the way down to Homer's Island. The doc's place sits right on the water, a boxy lookin' weatherboard bungalow with a big porch that looks out over the inlet. The air is salty and rich and I have to admit, the way it fills my lungs is revitalisin'. Brenda #4 goes inside and shoots straight for the kitchen. Within minutes, she's up to her elbows in corn starch, makin' the three of us lunch. The doc walks me around the back of the house to show me his boat.

'How's the old Johnson workin'?' he asks, right outta the blue.

'What?'

'Still havin' trouble gettin' it up for your wife?'

'I'm *not* havin' trouble gettin' it up. It's Brenda. She says stupid things in bed.'

'Alright, don't get worked up.'

'I ain't worked up. You don't understand. The other night she walks straight out of the bathroom, drops her towel and says "Now, Sweetiepie, I'd like you to plunder my quivering treasure."'

'She said that?'

'Yeah, she did. It always sounds rehearsed. I shrivel up like the last chicken in the shop.'

'Maybe she's done porn films. You ever check into her past?'

'She ain't done porn films, Doc. She went to actin' school in Trenton.'

'Sounds to me like she's done a few porn films. Here's my skiff,' he says, endin' the discussion abruptly.

The skiff is tied to a small landing, rockin' softly on the tide.

'Sixteen-foot Carolina,' he says. 'All fiberglass. Thirty-five-horsepower Evinrude.' He clambers down on to the dock, props a foot on it and strikes a pose, like he's just claimed land for the fuckin' queen or somethin'. I don't know a goddamn thing about boats. To me it looks like a shallow bathtub with a steerin' wheel in the middle.

'You wanna give it a run, Otis?'

'Maybe later.'

'Fine. We'll take it out first thing tomorrow. Your fluke is an early-mornin' fish.'

211

On the way back to the house, he says, 'Sometimes a person can be so real, you just don't wanna have sex with 'em. You need some imagined entity to create an atmosphere. Maybe both of you are foolin' yourselves.'

I think about that.

'What should I do?' I say.

'I'm no marriage counselor. But if it was me, I'd waste this one and start all over again.'

Which is exactly what I've been thinkin' lately.

That night, Brenda grills us a dinner of red snapper. We sit out on the porch and watch the nightboats drift up and down the inlet. He's courteous to Brenda but not overly conversational. Every time he looks at her, his face tightens, like he's thinkin' of some very private joke. Brenda's spent the day admirin' every facet of the doc's household. She clucked with joy at his modern kitchen. Clucked at his big TV. Clucked at his plush patio furniture. Clucked like a hen at roost all goddamn day. Now she seems serene as the warm breeze blows ripples across the inlet. I think about that lousy garden apartment with its uninvited mice. About how she pays all the rent, 'cause I'm broke. About how I haven't been on stage in almost a year, 'cause I've dried up creatively. I'm just not bringin' much to this party.

A boat creeps up the inlet with just its runner lights glowin' in the dark. We can hear a man's voice over the drone of the outboard, a raw Jersey voice.

'Dumb,' the voice is sayin'. 'Just fuckin' dumb. You let the fish ambush your fuckin' bait like that, you don't catch squat.' He seems to be chastising an unseen fishin' partner. 'With a fish, you gotta stuff it. You fake it outta its shoes. You gotta make a sincere effort to get in its face.'

The voice fades up the inlet, goin' on and on about Jersey-style take-no-prisoners fishin'.

A wave of homesickness washes over me. In the South, no one cares much about facial proximity.

Doc shows us the guest bedroom and calls it a night. We listen to him head down the stairs and when it's quiet, Brenda #4 goes into the guest bathroom and reappears in one of those slutty catalog negligees that only look good on svelte models. Her tits are pushin' it too forward and it hangs like a garbage bag. More disconcerting is the small white string trailin' out of her just below where the negligee ends.

'Surprise,' she says.

But I'm not surprised. I'm just lookin' at that string. She looks down and sees it, says 'Oops' and giggles. She walks up to me. She gets right in my face.

'We're not squeamish are we, Sugar?' she says. 'Go on, pull it out.'

'I don't really want to.'

'You think it's gonna explode like a party favour? Pull it.'

Somewhat reluctantly, I grasp it between my thumb and forefinger and tug. There's some resistance at first and then it plops out, danglin' between us in a way that makes me think of that mouse under her kitchen cupboard. I look around the room for a moment, then toss it out the window toward the inlet. It's not a gesture meant to look jaunty, but I guess it comes off that way 'cause she pushes me toward the bed and says, 'My ovaries are singin' like a lusty boat captain.'

'That's it!' I say, and duck underneath her before she can pin me to the bed. She wrinkles her face and looks at me quizzically.

'What does that mean, "that's it"?'

'It means whoever it is you're tryin' to be, it ain't workin'.'

213

'I'm tryin' to be a good wife. It's just that plain.'

'Maybe if you stopped *tryin'* . . . Just be yourself.'

'You don't want me as myself. You've made that clear. I don't know what you want.'

'To get out of New Jersey. I'm bored, Brenda. I'm just passin' time here. I need to start writin' and performin' again.'

She sits down on the edge of the bed, lookin' weary in her new negligee.

'Why don't we go to Tennessee?' I say.

'There's already a Dolly Parton in Tennessee.'

'Texas, then. Austin.'

'That's not gonna happen, Otis.'

She says that so curtly I know there's no point pushin' it.

'How is it,' she says, 'that you can love someone and not desire them?'

'I don't know,' I answer. And that's the truth. It's just the way it is.

That, I suppose, is your cold flame.

Doc gets me up early the followin' mornin'. There's eggs and bacon and strong coffee, and when we're done he practically bounds outside and down to the skiff. I follow him, tryin' to absorb some of his zest, but as far as I'm concerned, fishin' is just a grown man tryin' to trick an animal with a brain the size of a Cheerio.

I look up and see the darkened guest-room window. Brenda #4's still asleep in there. Our discussion from the night before looms like a hangover.

Doc gets all the tackle in and deposits himself at the console seat. I sit back by the outboard and we pull away, smooth green water passin' beneath us. He aligns the skiff into the breeze and drifts it out past a big desalinization plant, then out into the main channel of Barnegat Inlet. He starts makin' what he calls 'a two hook rig' on the fishin' line. He's tryin' to talk me through the lingo but it's all gibberish.

'This is splitshot,' he says. 'This will let the bait hook drag the bottom where the fluke can find it.'

He slips a bloody strip of bait on to the hook and hands the rod to me. I stare at it, dumbly.

'How can a country boy not know anything about fishin'?' he says.

'I led a sheltered childhood.'

He shows me how to throw the brake bar and cast, then drag the lure and set it.

'By some freak of nature,' he announces, 'fluke have both eyes on one side of their head.'

'Is that 'cause of all the refineries around here?'

'Nah, it's just a fluke!' he snorts.

'You promised no jokes, Doc.'

'Couldn't help myself. Anyway, you drag that bait right, they'll take it like nobody's business.'

'What is this?' I ask, holdin' the slithery bait in my palm.

'Squid. But fluke'll pounce on almost anything.'

We fish for almost an hour, workin' the same spot. I spend most of the time tryin' to perfect my cast. The doc is right: it is relaxin', even though I'm just castin', not really fishin'. Then Doc starts up the outboard and says we're movin' to a new spot. We head up the inlet, pickin' our way around other skiffs full of fishermen.

We stop, not twenty yards from another boat. There's two guys in it, talkin' at a volume most mothers use to call their kids in. I wonder if it's the boat we heard the previous night.

'I'll show these sonofabitches who's boss!' one of the loud-mouthed guys yells and rockets his lure into the water with

215

a vengeance. I can hear bottles and cans clatterin' from the bottom of their skiff. They've likely been drinkin' all night. Both look like extras from *Rocky*: leather jackets and open-necked shirts, gold neckchains and flashy watches. I'm surprised they're not just threatenin' the fish into givin' themselves up.

Doc suggests I move up to the bow, where I can cast toward the deep part of the inlet. I crawl past him awkwardly, tryin' not to capsize the boat.

'Easy,' he says, and gives me a forearm for support.

I take a seat on the bow and start to reach for the bait bucket when I notice Brenda #4's tampon lyin' indelicately on the floor of the boat. I reach down and pick it up by the string, tryin' not to let the doc see it. It leaves a rude smear on the skiff's gleaming white bottom. I start to plop it overboard into the water, but an idea stops me. I sink my hook into the fat squishy center and, with a flourish, whip the rod back and fire it toward the middle of the inlet. Why not? The doc said fluke will eat anything.

The breeze catches it and I watch with sickenin' dismay as it carries across the channel and lands smack-dab in the lap of the Loudmouth guy.

He stops mid-sentence and slowly tilts his head down toward his lap. I watch as his eyes follow the length of the line and settle, finally, on me. My innards tighten. I quickly snap my rod back, but I've forgotten to set the drag bar. The filament just wisps through the air and floats on the breeze. I set the brake and reel. Loudmouth disquietly observes the tampon crawl across his leg, snake over the gunwale and plop into the water.

Within seconds, he's started his skiff and the two goons are headin' toward us.

When they reach us I can see just how big both of them are. Loudmouth reaches a beefy hand out, grabs the edge

216

of our skiff and pulls himself alongside me. His face is right in my face. His face is roughly twice as large as my face.

'If that was what I think it was,' he says, 'we've got ourselves quite a little problem.'

'What's goin' on?' says the doc, oblivious.

'Tell your friend here we'd like to inspect his bait.'

I reel the bait in, each turn of the crank buildin' to what I know will be a painful finale. Suddenly there is a violent explosion of water and a huge fluke shoots upward, bulging at both eyes, which, true to Doc's word, are on the same side of its head like a Picasso painting. The fish makes a swift run away from the boat, then flags almost immediately. The two thugs watch with amazement as I reel it in, Doc nets it and drops it into the boat. The doc says it probably weighs a good fifteen pounds.

Suitably impressed, Loudmouth feels there's no further need of kickin' ass and the two of them skirr off down the inlet.

Back at Doc's place, Brenda #4 sets a huge platter of fresh fluke, baked in cornmeal batter, on to the dining-room table. The doc digs right in, savourin' every morsel. Brenda's high spirits from the day before have given way to a polite stupor. She nibbles disconsolately. I tell them I'm not hungry and munch on some potato salad.

Then Brenda #4 says she ought to get back to Atlantic City in time for her show and the doc walks us out to her car.

'I've never seen you more relaxed,' he says to me and slaps me on the back. 'I think you're on your way.'

He gives Brenda #4 a cursory kiss goodbye on the cheek and watches us pull away.

Brenda doesn't say anything to me the whole trip, just

drives and pouts. All the while, my favorite Dolly Parton song is goin' through my head: 'Tennessee Homesick Blues'. We head down the Parkway in silence, turn right after the big bridge at Absecon and head east. But in my thoughts, I'm already headed west.

I never did catch that goddamned mouse.

Brenda #5

All I had to show for two years of marriage was one song.
I don't remember writin' it, but when the bourbonitis fog
cleared, there it was, my legacy of two years of blind
marriage:

Do you remember nights beneath the Milky Way?
I held you in my arms and darlin' how we'd sway
And lean against
That old wood fence
Or a tree trunk

I guess I said I loved you 'bout a million times
Felt the earth go spinnin' when you said that
You'd be mine
Do you remember?
Well I don't
'Cause I was drunk!

I held you oh so many nights it seemed just like a fog
I'd stroke your head I'd say good girl
Might've thought you were my dog

A springer spaniel, that Old Jack Daniel's
How far I've sunk
And I used to write you love poems all the time
You said it didn't matter
That the rhyming scheme was awkward
Do you remember?
Well I don't
'Cause I was drunk

Did we have kids? I don't remember
Did we get married in October or September?
Ain't it funny how the alcohol
Just don't affect the heart at all?

'Cause darlin' in this sober light
You're lookin' just as pretty
And I haven't touched a drink
Since we left Atlantic City

Now the ocean breeze is rustlin'
And the sun is sinking orange
And I'd like to make a rhyme right now
But I painted myself into a corner
Do you remember?
I don't
'Cause I was drunk!!

I took that song to Austin, Texas and started poundin'
the sidewalk. I was fairly sober now and full of determi-
nation. I played the honky-tonks and chili parlors up and
down 6th Street. Every alleyway blew its beery breath in
my face. Much like my Old Man, I offered myself up to
every form of self-abuse available: songwriter-in-the-round

220

gigs, amateur nights, gong shows, coffee houses. I plied my small arsenal of songs, 'I was Drunk', 'Women Call It Stalking', 'Battered-Women's Shelter', 'Crawl Inside a Bottle' and 'Baby You're Blue' to drunks, college kids, cowboys and drifters.

Beyond 6th Street, unobstructed, the University of Texas tower rose like a carbine shell – the ghost of a nutcake sniper named Charles Whitman perched at the top, squinting through a rifle scope and sayin' 'I can get 'em from here'. The exit ramps were full of hitchhikers with guitar cases, guys who'd given up on their dream. Well, not me. No fuckin' way.

And then one night I finally caught a break.

It happened in a honky-tonk called the Pair-a-Dice. I'd just finished a set and collected fourteen dollars and some change from the pass-around bucket. I was feelin' pretty happy with myself for just tryin' out a new song, which dealt with the subtle indiscretions of a cheatin' woman. It was called 'The Scrabble Song':

> You coulda played HEART
> The word was right there from the start
> But you rearranged the letters
> And it came out HATER
> You coulda played CHASTE
> But you let my good love go to waste
> Put your tits in someone else's face
> So why don't you play CHEATS?
>
> You coulda gave me ROSES
> But you just gave me SORES
> I could put down SHOWER
> But you stay gone for hours
> So, I think I'll play WHORES

221

You coulda played LOVE
But you played EVOL
Who the hell taught you to spell?
But its evil just as well

You coulda played BEDROOM and PLEASE
But you played BOREDOM and ASLEEP
And I don't need these ACRIMONIES
So I'm movin' to MICRONESIA

You coulda played HEART
The word was right there from the start
But you rearranged the letters
And it came out HATER

I was sittin' at the bar with my buddy, a rodeo clown named Chesty Laporte. Since I'd arrived in Austin, Chesty had kind of taken me under his wing. A rodeo clown's job consists of crawlin' into steel barrels to distract bulls from riders, then emergin' to do balloon tricks. It was a schizo occupation and Chesty dealt with it by drinkin' and fightin' as much as he possibly could. We were engaged in our usual argument which had to do with whether Chesty was an athlete or an entertainer. He felt, quite strongly, he was an athlete. I would remind him that he wore his underwear outside his pants and shot bottle rockets from his ass for a finale. That, to me, said 'entertainer'.

Suddenly, there was a tap on my shoulder and I turned around to see Narvel Crump. That's right, Narvel Crump. The wax-shouldered, slab-faced country corn-pone heart-throb who'd once fleeced my second wife for everything she owned.

'I liked your stuff up there,' he said. 'I'm Narvel Crump.'
He extended a manicured hand.

222

'Otis,' I said. 'What're ya drinkin?'

We ordered bourbons all 'round.

The three of us drank and Narvel exuded his oleaginous charm on everyone around, shakin' hands, signin' autographs, puttin' out 'aw shucks' vibes. I'd never been around anyone famous before, unless you count Brenda #4, who, when she was Dolly Parton, emitted minor celebrity wattage no more powerful than a wax-museum figure. Sitting with Narvel, I felt weirdly illuminated, like bein' caught in headlights. With his toothy grin and broad, stockman's shoulders, I could see how dumb women found him attractive.

'That "Scrabble Song" is a real hoot,' he said. 'I could do something with that song.'

'Yeah, steal it,' is what I thought. The same way he'd stolen Brenda #2's furniture. Chesty listenin' in, promptly appointed himself my representative.

'That song's hot,' he said, fanning his collar.

'I believe it's currently tied up in some sort of bidding war, ain't that right, Otis?'

'Who's this?' said Narvel.

'Chesty Laporte,' he said. 'I'm in entertainment . . .'

A minute ago he was an athlete.

'. . . and it's a pleasure, Narvel, to be in your certified eminence.' What an ass-kisser!

'Well, that song's gettin' there,' said Narvel. 'I'm lookin' for something frivolous to put on my next album.'

Frivolous? I'd spilled my guts on that song.

"Course I'd do a few minor changes on the lyrics,' he added. 'It's a little salty.' He gave me a level gaze.

'What d'ya say? Wanna sell it?'

'I don't know,' I said.

'We both of us know,' said Narvel, 'there's no balance sheet and five-year plan in this business. If I record one of your songs, your foot's in the door.' He motioned around the room. 'Half the shitkickers in this town would sell their momma to have me record one of their songs. You ought to think about it real serious.'

'Otis has an eye toward recordin' that song himself,' said Chesty.

Narvel regarded Chesty like a fly on his eggs. The fact that Chesty still had rouge on his cheeks from a matinee rodeo probably wasn't helpin' his credibility.

'What if I hook you up with some session boys I know and I produce your album? On my label.'

I was thinkin' back to the songs I'd heard Narvel sing, and you know what? They weren't all that bad. I mean, the man had found his niche. We all gotta find our niche.

'You'll need at least ten songs,' Narvel said.

'Oh, he's got a buttload of songs,' said Chesty.

'Well, do we have a deal? You give me 'The Scrabble Song'. I make you an album.'

I knew if I didn't say yes, he would steal the song anyway – step all over me and there wouldn't be much I could do about it. So I said, 'Alright.'

'Great!' said Chesty, smackin' his shot glass against the table. 'From here on in, Narv, you'll be dealin' directly with me. Our boy here will be very busy polishing his repertoire.'

I needed a few weeks to hammer out enough songs to fill an album. I was livin', temporarily, on Chesty's couch. He owned a French poodle and a Shetland pony, both part of his rodeo act. He kept them indoors, where they wandered listlessly from room to room, like a couple of old men. Most mornings I would wake up on the couch with the pony

224

eyein' me glumly, waitin' to be fed his oats. Thankfully, Chesty took off on the circuit for a spell and left me with some peace and quiet.

'Write what you know.' That's the songwriter's supreme advice. Well, what did I know? Prison and romance. I thought there might be a niche for romantic prison songs. So I wrote a song called 'He Almost Looks Like You'.

There's a full moon
Shinin' on a stainless toilet bowl
An eight-by-twelve room
Shrinks every time that I'm denied parole
It was a s.n.a.f.u.
Now I'm missin' you and holed up in this pen
And there's a tattoo
On my ass that says that I belong to him

My cellmate beats me black 'n' blue
But in the dark it's true
He almost looks like you

It's never hello
He just knocks me to the ground and then he strikes me
But when he gives me jello
In the dinin' hall at night I know he likes me
I'd never kiss him
But sometimes I feel the urge to lie beside him
Guess I would miss him
If they took him down the hall and they fried him

Though he beats me black 'n' blue
In the dark it's true
He almost looks like you

And I just mind my place
Well, I don't want no trouble
But girl he's got your face
Save for a quarter inch of stubble

Now my heart's broke
And I'm missin' you so much it makes me tremble
It's God's joke
To put me in a cell with someone you resemble
And he's a creep
When he tries to force himself on other fellas
But down deep, I must admit I get a little jealous
When he says that I'm the one for him
Then he sneaks off with other men
He almost looks like you
Yeah he almost looks like you.

I wasn't sure how that one was goin' to sit with the more conservative listeners. Little did I know it would become a real showstopper.

The other prison song I wrote wasn't so upbeat. It had to do with the romantic fixations that develop after you've spent too much time behind bars. It was called, simply, 'Glass'.

Hello, Glass. Good to see you my old pal
You remember the woman
Used to sit right across from where I'm sittin' now
I used to speak to her through you
Put my cheek to you
Stroke your surface
Till the guards got nervous
Oh Glass
It's good to see you my old friend

Because a man gets used to anything
Inside this cage where birds don't sing
And to feel the thrill of cheap perspex
Is the closest that he'll come to sex
And when they let me out of here
You were nowhere to be found

There was a plate-glass window
In a motel room in Santa Fe
Well I got a little drunk
A little wistful, a little carried away
And what I call a slight loss of composure
The cops called 'indecent exposure'
So Glass, I'm back
It's good to see you my old friend

Because a man gets used to anything
Inside this cage where birds don't sing

The reference to Santa Fe in that song felt a little artificial
'cause I'd never actually been to Santa Fe, but any singer
knows that along with San Antonio, Dallas, Fort Worth and
any town in Oklahoma, it's a requisite country music name
check.

Narvel invited me to one of his shows and afterwards, backstage. He was surrounded by a clutch of lapdog well-wish-
ers and sycophants who clung to him like Christmas tinsel.
He called 'em 'Narvellites'.

'You're authentic, Otis,' he said, slappin' my shoulder.
'Stay outta Nashville. You want some advice? *Stayoutta-
nashville!* That place was stealin' my soul.'

I figured he'd probably pillaged Nashville for everything it could offer and had to move his tent to Austin.

Still, I smiled and played along. Even a dog can shake hands.

I cut my album in a day and a half. Thankfully, as producer, Narvel didn't force his schmaltzy imprint on my songs. He was, as they say, strictly hands off. So hands off he never bothered to turn up. The session guys he saddled me with showed the work ethic of substitute teachers. They would listen to me play a song, turn on the tape machine and mechanically churn out the same half-cooked fillips, noodlings, and ribbony steel guitar runs you've heard on a million disposable country tunes.

'Earthier', 'Swampier' I'd instruct them, after each bland take. I couldn't seem to find the right word to convey what I wanted. They'd nod their heads, smile tightly to suppress a yawn and play the same goddamn thing as before. In other words, they stuck a hat and spurs on it and called it a day.

A few weeks later, Narvel called. I thought he wanted to talk about my album, but he didn't mention it. He wanted me to come out to his house the followin' night for some wingding he was throwin' to celebrate his new single: 'The Scrabble Song'.

'Put your best hat on,' he said. 'You're goin' places, buddy.'

I didn't have a hat.

I brought Chesty along. On the drive over, we did some calculatin'. We figured there were maybe six hundred country and western stations in the country. If they put 'The Scrabble Song' into their rotation, it would get played six, maybe eight times a day. A songwriter gets a nickel every time his song is played. That came out to two hundred dollars a day, twice as much as what Chesty made for crouching inside a barrel. I felt damned good.

We headed out of Austin north, where the roadside was furred with bluebonnets and Indian paint-brush. The hitch-hikers, with their slung guitars, were everywhere and I couldn't help feelin' elevated, that my days as a shitkicker were behind me.

Narvel had bought himself an old ranch house up near Kerrville. The house was covered in rose-cluttered trellises, indicatin' a woman in his life. It was shaded in a stand of cedar trees and surrounded by lush, carefully tended pasture. A couple of well-groomed horses grazed in a corral next to a brand new, hand-timbered barn. The initials NC had been emblazoned in brand-style letterin' across the doors. There were dozens of vehicles parked outside the house, at slapdash angles. We were in Chesty's Toyota, a battered pickup with a derelict camper shell on the back that served as his bedroom on the road, in those rare cases where he couldn't find some drunken roadhouse trollop to shack-up with for the night. All these shiny, expensive rigs parked everywhere made us *both* feel like rodeo clowns.

We could hear voices and loud music as we approached. Chesty rang the doorbell and poked me in the ribs, as if to say, 'Here we go!'. We waited. He rang the bell again. The door parted and there stood Brenda #2, my ex-wife.

All I could think to say was the first thing I'd ever said to her.

'How ya doin', Sizzlechest?' I shouted, a bit too cavalier for even Chesty's sense of decorum.

Man, was she ever startled.

'Well, whaddya know,' she said. She hugged me, then pushed me away to have a good look.

'You two know each other?' said Chesty.

'Yeah, we know each other,' I said.

She still smelled like cinnamon and butter. A pair of golden retrievers bounded up the hallway toward us and when Brenda bent down to gather them in her arms, I knew she lived there.

Narvel appeared in a big white Stetson and a shiny silver belt buckle the size of a dinner plate. He wrapped his arms around Brenda's waist and swayed her around the hallway.

'Meet Brenda, my fiancée,' he said, and nuzzled her neck. As he manhandled her, she gave me a look clearly meant to indicate she'd never mentioned me to Narvel.

The dogs' noses were all over Chesty's crotch, sensing traces of livestock.

'Well, don't just stand in the hallway,' Narvel called out. 'Get in here and help us put a dent in some chili!'

Narvel led us into a livin' room where the get-together was in full swing. I recognized a few of the faces from Narvel's backstage gatherin'. Chesty honed in on a fish tank full of Everclear punch. A handful of revelers were gathered around it and one guy, an agent type in a velvet shirt, was swallowin' red peppers, apparently on a dare. His hair sweated and his face looked inflamed. With waning bravado, he espoused on every Texan's favorite subject: Texas.

'Austin's the only one ain't ruined somehow. You can forget 'bout Dallas and you can forget 'bout Fort Worth.' He wiped his face with his shirtsleeve. 'And as for Houston, highest unreported murder rate in the US of A.'

'How do you know?' asked Chesty, jumpin' right in.

'Know what?' said Pepperface.

'If it's unreported, how do you know it was a murder?'

Pepperface looked confused. He shoved a finger in Chesty's chest.

'Don't get smart,' he said.

'Keep that up,' Chesty growled, lookin' at the man's finger.

I grabbed him and steered him away from the fish tank. We walked into a cedar-paneled den where Narvel's framed gold records lined the walls. The room was full of people watching a television that, strangely, sat upside down.

'You need to see this,' someone said, and handed me a beer.

They were watchin' a video of *The Poseidon Adventure*, the capsize scene. The ship's passengers floated spectrally upward while the furniture stuck to the floor. When the scene cut to Shelley Winters thrashing about in a Christmas tree, a cheer rose up from the entire room and glasses were clinked all around.

I left Chesty there and wandered out, hopin' to catch Brenda #2 alone. I wanted to ask her why in hell she'd gone back to Narvel, after everything she'd once told me about him.

I found her in the kitchen, stirrin' the chili. She was wearin' a studded denim jacket and matchin' skirt and those calves were as fine as ever. Hell, she looked better than when *I* was married to her. Her skin was lustrous. No doubt, she'd been sand-blasted by an expensive dermatologist. She looked up and gave me an off-center smile.

'Congratulations,' she said.

'On what?'

'Big-time songwriter.'

'Oh yeah.'

I went right up beside her and watched her stir. For a moment, I sensed a mutual awkwardness. Suddenly she grabbed my hand and said, 'Come outside.'

I followed her out past the barn to the corral. She leaned up against a fence-rail.

'That's Copy, short for Copper Miner's daughter,' she said, pointing out the larger horse.

'She's a foxtrotter. And the white one is called Wesley. They're both gaited.'

'What are you doin' with an asshole like Narvel Crump?' I said.

'I was gonna ask you the same thing.'

'I don't know,' I said. 'I ain't exactly been inundated with offers.'

'Well, me neither to tell you the truth.' She smiled again, 'I suppose it's the illusion of everlasting happiness.'

'Illusion.'

'Besides, the West is where it all begins, isn't that what they say?' Then she said, 'Maybe after you break up with someone, the good memories have a longer shelf life than the bad ones. So you forget why you broke up and go back. I went back.'

'You have good memories of us?'

'You're still carryin' a torch for me, aren't you?' she said, almost proudly.

'I guess I am.'

She leaned against my shoulder.

'Well, whaddya know. The old flame.'

I put my hand on her ass. She didn't try to move it.

'You should be flattered,' I said. 'Not everyone has such a warm view of the past.'

'Put your warm view away. Here comes my fiancé.'

Narvel was walkin' out toward us. He *had* to wonder what his future wife was doin' out here with a man she'd only just met. I wondered if he'd seen my hand on her ass.

He came up and draped his arms across Brenda's shoulders.

'Whaddya think of the steeds?' said Narvel, belying nothin'.

'Nice horses,' I answered.

'That little Appaloosa will steer like a sports car. Taught

her to neck rein myself. Smooth as a fart through silk.'

'Well, I don't know much about horses,' I said.

He rocked Brenda back and forth with the weight of his body.

'Restraint,' he said.

'What?'

'*Restraint*. A good horse goes where it's led.'

He swung Brenda around to where she was between us. Over her shoulder, he narrowed his gaze at me.

'Otherwise, it ends up as dog-food.'

The party got rowdier. Chesty was runnin' around administering grain alcohol shots to all. Pepperface had tied his belt around the golden retrievers' legs, joinin' them together.

'Look, Siamese dogs,' he yelled, drunkenly.

Narvel's bass player, wearin' a T-shirt that read 'Linoleum-cutters do it on the floor', had cajoled a dozen people into a game of 'Beer Hunter'. He would shake a warm can of beer and shuffle it around with five or six other cans. The players took turns pickin' a can, holdin' it up to their ear and crackin' it open. A woman with silver coyotes for earrings warned everyone her brother had got a 'yeast infection in his ear from these kind of shenanigans'. Pepperface replied that he'd rather have yeast in his ear than those 'cheap gadgets hangin' off your jug-handles'. Then he unloaded a volley of hot foam right into the side of her face. I looked over and saw Narvel draggin' Brenda forcefully down a hallway and into a bedroom. The door slammed shut behind them.

Eventually, Narvel reappeared and herded us all into his music room to play his new recording of 'The Scrabble Song'. He introduced me all around as the song's writer.

'Otis here just cut an album, y'all!' he announced, fiddlin' with the CD player. There were cursory murmurs from the group. 'In my studio,' he added. He looked at me. 'I extended him that courtesy.'

'What you gonna call it?' someone asked.

'*My Donuts, Goddamn,*' I said.

'What kinda dumbass name is that for a record?' squawked Pepperface.

I explained that at the end of Lynyrd Skynyrd's 'Sweet Home Alabama', Ronnie Van Zandt can clearly be heard exclaiming that phrase as he's watchin' the engineer in the sound booth eat his precious Krispy Kremes.

'Worst title ever,' someone said.

'I like it,' came Brenda's voice, from behind me. I turned to see her leanin' in the doorway. Narvel's imprint, in the shape of a hand, burned across the side of her face. I looked back at Narvel. He was giving her a dead stare. Brenda backed out of the doorway and disappeared.

Narvel said he'd taken a few liberties with the 'theme' of 'The Scrabble Song' and pressed the play button on the CD player. I sat down on a piano bench and listened in horror to what he'd done to my song:

> You coulda' played HATER
> The word was right there from the start
> But you rearranged the letters
> And it came out HEART
>
> I've always played my BETS
> But this time I gave you my BEST
> The love for you that I have carried
> Went from ADMIRER straight to MARRIED
>
> I saw CANOES but you saw OCEANS
> An endless sea of pure devotion

> So darlin' take me as I am
> Not CALM but happy as a CLAM . . .

At that point in the song, lush, turgid, orchestral strings were swelling under the lyrics and my brain just went numb.

We all sat down in the dinin' room to chili. People talked to me and I nodded absently, not really hearin'. My brain was screamin' over what Narvel had done to my song. 'Fuck this music business,' I thought. It's as fuckin' petty as any crime I'd ever committed. All I wanted to do was grab Brenda and drive away with her, far past the Texas State Line.

Narvel was holdin' vicious sway over the guests, recounting a story about one of Brenda's friends.

'I come home one afternoon, and there's Naydra, languid on the sofa. She's had a few in her and she's tanked, right? Brenda's not home, out shoppin', whatever. Well, don't you know Naydra starts *comin' on to me*! She's unbuttoning her blouse. In our house!'

He grabbed Brenda's hand and brought it up to his, lacing his fingers with hers. Brenda smiled weakly. The handprint on her face had faded, but it was still there, a harsh blotch. Narvel was clearly soused.

'Well, I marched straight out to my truck! I mean, this is Brenda's best friend we're talkin' about! Allofasudden Brenda come wheelin' up in her car. I go back inside and say "Naydra, button up your shirt for Chrissakes, Brenda's here!" And Naydra's laughin'. She's not really drunk at all. She say's "Narvel, this was a little infidelity test I cooked up, 'cause Brenda's my best friend and I'm lookin' out for her interests. And you just passed!" Then she gives me a big hug. Tells me how happy she is for me 'n' Brenda.'

Narvel paused for a genial response from everyone. Brenda just looked stunned with embarrassment.

235

'So the moral there . . .' Narvel said, pausing to swig from the Everclear, '. . . is *always* keep your condoms in your truck!'

Narvel's sycophants all laughed in unison. The others stared into their chili. Brenda's eyes welled up with tears.

Then Chesty leapt up from the table and went straight for Narvel Crump.

There's no point in goin' into the minute details of the ensuing brawl. Chesty pinned Narvel to the floor and a lot of non-specific punches got thrown all around. Someone managed to separate the two. They dragged Narvel to a chair in the music room and Chesty got pushed to the kitchen where he kept braying, 'Bring on the pain!' Anyone should know better than to get on the wrong side of a clown.

Brenda and me ended up outside in the driveway.

'Maybe it's none of my business . . .' I started to say.

'Oh you've made it your business alright.'

'. . . but, I just don't see it between you two.'

'What would you know?' she said bitterly. 'Your song, by the way, is wretched.'

'That ain't my song! My version had some bite to it.'

She was lookin' around at all the guests' cars.

'Let's take one of these for a ride.'

'I ain't stealin' no one's car,' I said.

'This from the man who once took my own trailer from underneath me. What have you turned into?'

'What have *you* turned into?'

'I don't know,' she said. She was cryin' now. I put my arm around her.

I asked her if she remembered the last thing she'd said to me when I was in prison.

'What did I say?'

236

'You said you wished we'd had a chance to make it work.'
'The chances were Slim and None. And Slim left town.'
'Slim's back in town.'
'I need to go somewhere to think,' she said.
'We ought to go somewhere to fuck,' I said.
'Pure poetry. You really must be a crackerjack lyricist.'
She crawled out from under my arm, went over to a BMW
and peered into the driver's window.

'C'mon, Otis,' she said, 'pick one.'

I found us a nice Ford pickup with the keys still in the ignition and we went somewhere to think – roughly a thousand
miles away.

Lake Mead

Ask me what it's like to be dead.

Peaceful. Pure relief. No IRS after me. No process servers or lawyers wantin' alimony payments. No federal agents wantin' to talk to me about the fact I never got around to officially divorcin' any of my various wives. No Narvel Crump tryin' to kill me. Once I was dead, all those problems just floated off into the ether.

Brenda #2 and me drove to Las Vegas. She got a job waitressin' and I found work playin' piano for a country cover band called The Grubstakes.

We moved into a motel called The Alhambra, on the Strip right up from the Sahara. I bought an old Ford pickup that had been bleached gray by the desert sun, but reliable. One night we caught Don Rickles at the Tropicana, then drove to a stucco Wed-O-Mat and Brenda #2 became Brenda #5.

I'd called Chesty when I first got to Vegas. He promised me he was gonna lean on Narvel and make sure my record got released. Sure enough, I went into Tower Records one afternoon and there was a single copy of *My Donuts, Goddamn* in the Country section, right between Billy 'Crash' Craddock and Rodney Crowell. Every day for a week I went in to look at my album, and then one day it was gone. I felt pure elation.

I kept an eye on the country music sales chart in *Billboard*. But I never saw any mention of *My Donuts, Goddamn*. The day The Grubstakes introduced Narvel Crump's big hit, 'The Scrabble Song', into their set list, I packed up my guitar and left without a word. Maybe that was rude, but equally as rude was Brenda leavin', which is what happened that very afternoon.

I went back to the motel room and she was foldin' her clothes and puttin' them in a holdall.

'What's goin' on?' I said.

'A process server came by here a little while ago.'

'Here?'

'Yes, here.'

I went over to the curtain and peered out. How could he have found me in a run-down motel in Las Vegas?

'What did he want?'

'There were two of them actually. You've been a very inattentive little boy. When were you gonna mention your last coupla wives? *Undivorced wives.*'

'It's somethin' I've been meanin' to clear up.'

'You don't say. Seems you've got quite a collection of warm memories you haven't told me about.'

She threw the last few clothes in the bag.

'I can straighten this out.'

'I'll be in the bathroom.' She went in and shut the door behind her.

Not the bathroom again, I thought. How come my marriages never went down the *kitchen* drain?

I went over and pushed the door open. She was throwin' cosmetics into a plastic shopping bag.

'You ain't gotta go,' I said.

'Oh, I do.'

'But why? I don't understand.'

She turned to me furiously.

'Here's why. Because marriage isn't good for you, Otis. Because you're sloppy at it. You're a deserter and a no-show, and you can't treat people like that! You can't treat *me* like that.'

'I haven't.'

'But you *will*. I'm not your newest "source of inspiration" or something to reflect on like a fucking mirror. You'll go through me like water, like you did the others. Unh uh. No. Fuck you.'

'It's not gonna be like that,' I said, but it sounded as hollow as I guess it really was. I felt like I'd just been burned alive. By her description of me. By her pure, genuine rage.

'I need somethin' permanent,' she said.

Then she pushed past me and left.

I couldn't blame her. I realized by now I was always gonna be on parole from 'Love'. Or whatever it is the kids are callin' it these days.

I'd been askin' around about George Lively. I'd found out from someone at the Sahara that he'd got his settlement. He'd moved down to a place called Oatman, Arizona, a quasi-ghost town south of Hoover Dam.

I drove down there to find him. I crossed over the vast spillway of Hoover Dam. Lake Mead stretched out in all directions, green and glorious. Crimson bluffs rose up from the shoreline, luminous in the heat. The shadows of clouds shot across them like guillotines. It was one of the most magnificent things I'd ever seen and it cheered me up immensely, feelin', as I did, that all my consequences were rapidly addin' up to zero.

I stopped to take the tour of Hoover Dam. The guide told us all about how it had been built, the taming of the mighty Colorado, so on and so on. I asked him if anyone had ever fallen over the spillway.

'No one's lived to brag about it,' he said.

After the tour I went into the visitors' center and called Chesty collect.

'I'm glad you called,' he said. 'You want the bad news or the bad news?'

'Bad news first.'

'The bad news is you got a generous royalty check for 'The Scrabble Song' sittin' here.'

'Why is that bad news?'

'Narvel wants you to write more songs for him.'

'Oh.'

'He says no hard feelin's. Says you're welcome to Brenda.'

'What's the bad news?'

'There's a lien notice here from the IRS. They'd really like to hear from you.'

'Tell 'em I'm dead.'

'Tell who you're dead?'

'Everyone.'

'For how long?'

'A while. I'll let you know.'

'Great idea. That should give your album the push it needs.'

'Yeah.'

'Alright then. Tear it up, wild man!'

I got in my truck. Instead of headin' for Oatman, I turned north up a forest service road and drove along that for a while till it began to skirt the bluffs. I found a spot that looked out over the lake, stopped the truck, grabbed my guitar case and climbed out. I gazed across to where some sedan boats were cruising along a small blue arm that curved up into a canyon. I could just make out the figures on the boat.

I lit a cigarette, took a coupla drags and then pulled my guitar from the case. As precisely as possible, I burned *Otis Lee Crenshaw* into the wood, right below the soundhole.

Then I walked over to the cliff. Below me, the water brought my Old Man's ashes suddenly to mind. I wondered if they'd ever made it to Africa.

Then I slung the guitar back and hurled it away from the cliff. It tumbled end over end for what seemed like a long, long time, then hit the water makin' a clean, silent shock wave.

It wasn't like spankin' a six-year-old in the audience, but it seemed country crazy enough.

I left my guitar case full of songs on the hood and the truck keys in the ignition and headed back down the dirt track toward Oatman.

Brenda #6

Whaddya want, a nice, countrified endin'? Okay here's one:

Things were never the same after Brenda #5 left. The old silver mine outside of town shut down and the swimmin' hole dried up. The cattle all died from a brucellosis virus that was goin' 'round and Preacher Wilson caught consumption and passed away in the autumn.

Aunt Sally kept makin' Sunday dinners with that delicious apple sauce she always served, but folks just stopped comin' around to eat: we're all so busy nowadays, what with satellite dishes and home schoolin' and that spankin' new shoppin' mall just out past where the old grain silo used to stand.

Cousin Earl drove his pickup into a ditch and he never quite recovered from the head injury. The doctors said it was a miracle he survived at all. These days he just sits on the porch whittlin' bird whistles out of birchwood.

The drought hit and the bank went under and most days now I just sit in this old rockin' chair playin' five-cent pinochle with Festus from across the alley, who likes to hum *The Battle Hymn of the Republic* under his breath and sip corn likker from a Mason jar.

Someday, I reckon, a strong wind is gonna come and blow all this away.

There. That countrified enough for you?

'Course, none of that happened. I got myself a nice, suitably filthy little trailer down in Oatman, Arizona, three units over from George Lively. When I arrived, he never looked happier to see anyone in his whole life. He was convinced he had some kind of wastin'-away disease. One night he got all maudlin on me and made me promise when the time came, to 'put him out of his misery'. He claimed he was 'too chicken-shit' to do it himself. I felt really uncomfortable about the whole thing, but he sort of backed me into a corner. He told me I was the only person in the whole world he felt close to. He gave me a silver-plated Charter Arms .38 with a bullet in it and showed me where he wanted me to plug him – one clean shot right to the temple. Believe me, the whole thing freaked me out so much I spent all my time tryin' to avoid him.

I'd see him in a bar across the room and he'd lurch right over. He was still a little curvy from all the hip operations and walked kind of like Quasimodo.

'A promise is a promise, right Otis?' he'd say, and I'd reply, 'Sure thing, George,' hopin' he didn't want me to do it right then, not in the middle of a good bourbon with the baseball on the TV.

Then, to everyone's surprise, he got better. Whatever was eatin' away at him just stopped. He got kind of quasi-religious and new-agey on me and now he's always goin' on and on about daily affirmations and angels lookin' over him. I still have his gun and I'm seriously thinkin' about usin' it on him.

*   *   *

246

As for Brenda #5, well hell – the world is full of Brendas, ain't it? Just yesterday, I met this good-lookin' gal standin' on the wooden porch outside Oatman's only gas station. She was scratchin' off Lotto tickets. I came out from buyin' cigarettes and saw her there, barefoot in a cowboy shirt with the tail out. I'd seen her around town a few times.

I lit up a cigarette and watched her as she *partially* uncovered each scratch-off ticket, then tossed it into a trash can.

'Pardon me for bein' nosy,' I said, politely.

'Hello,' she said.

'You're not scratchin' off the whole ticket.'

'I know.'

She smiled and I could see she was good around the eyes. Dark and electric, with tiny crowsfeet which, these days, I find strangely alluring.

'How do you expect to win the sixty-one-million-dollar jackpot if you don't play the whole card?' I asked.

'I don't care about winnin',' she answered. 'I just enjoy watchin' the numbers unfold. If those first three numbers match, I quit right there.'

'Why?'

'The odds after that are astronomical. But I spend the afternoon imaginin' what it would be like if I really *had* won the jackpot. Which is nice to imagine.'

'Fuck me,' I thought, 'the world is turnin' lousy with new-age drivel.' But like I said, she had electrifyin' eyes.

A few yards away, a blue truck blared its horn. I looked over and saw a cowboy in the driver's seat, glarin' at her, impatiently.

'Brenda, get in the goddamned truck now!' he growled.

'Here we go again,' I thought.

'The possibility,' she said, winkin' at me, 'is always more rewardin' than the payoff.'

247

Then she padded over and climbed into the truck and I watched her drive away with the cowboy.

I thought about what she'd said. That it's okay if somethin' don't turn out to be a jackpot, because that wasn't the point in the first place. You just got to accept that.

I knew I'd go lookin' for her.

Just as soon as I was done fishin' through that trash can.